About

C000060624

Marion Cunningham was born and brought up in Walthamstow, East London, during the 1940/50s. She came from a large close knit family and had a very happy childhood. Most of her school holidays were spent with her maternal grandparents and without them this book could never have been written. She was also a constant visitor to their home throughout the coming years. Now widowed she lives on Canvey Island, Essex.

1

Authors note.

I am most fortunate for having had the opportunity to sit for many hours as a child and as a young woman, listening while my grandparents reminisced and recalled the many events that had taken place during their long lives.

Writing this book as a tribute to them has given me great pleasure and hopefully a lasting memory for their descendants present and future. Other readers, especially those with Bethnal Green and Walthamstow connections, may find this to be an interesting account of how life was for many prior to the First World War and the years that followed.

Based on a true account of events that happened and places that did at one time exist, many mentioned in this book are still standing today. In some parts a little fabrication and imagination was needed to fill the missing gaps.

Marion Cunningham January 2014
In the Centenary year of the start of The Great War of 1914

To Roger.
Best Wishes from

Marion Cunningham

He took the King's Shilling

FOR THE LOVE OF AMELIA

Marion Cunningham

www.fortheloveofamelia.co.uk

Front Cover:
Background picture taken in the trenches of France
Jesse Frederick Warren
Amelia with daughters Elizabeth and Beatrice
Cover Illustration by Lana Ann Yearley.

www.fast-print.net/store.php

For the Love of Amelia: He took the kings shilling
Copyright © Marion Cunningham 2014

A catalogue record for this book is available from the British Library

ISBN 978-178035-788-1

First published 2014 by
FASTPRINT PUBLISHING
Peterborough, England.

Acknowledgements

My sincere thanks go to my late mother Elizabeth Amelia Warren who throughout her life was always known as 'Milly'. She had the most wonderful memory and without her knowledge of dates, places and events long since passed, many details in this book would have simply been lost in time. She passed away in 2008 during her 96th year.

Thanks to my son Roy who has always shared my interest and for accompanying me to the War Graves and Battlefields of France and Belgium. Also for his account of the Battle of the Somme as seen through his great grandfather's eyes and for his detailed maps showing the movements of the Queen's Royal West Surrey's during the first two days of that terrible conflict.

I am also grateful to the Commanders War Diaries from the Public Record Office and for the retrieving of my Grandfathers Army Records from the 'Burnt Collection' by the Ministry of Defence.

Thanks to my son Paul who helped me with his technical and computer knowledge that often baffled me and to my granddaughter Lana for her assistance with arranging family photographs and for illustrating the cover of this book.

To my brother David with whom I often walk down Memory Lane.

To my granddaughter Ria who gave me confidence to write this book and to all my family including my daughter Debbie, daughter-in-law Jane and lifelong friend Maureen Shanks for their encouragement and interest.

Prologue

Part One

This book is based on the true story of Jesse Fredrick Warren a 24 year old French Polisher by trade who was living in Bethnal Green, East London with his wife Amelia and their two young daughters Elizabeth and Beatrice.

The start of the Great War in 1914 brought with it an end to regular employment and the beginning of great hardships for Jesse and his young family. By the February of 1915 they were destitute and starving. There was no money for food, gas or coal. Like so many other young men who found themselves in the same situation, there was only one option open to him: without telling his wife he signed on and volunteered for the Army. It was not for King and Country that he joined up but to put food on the table for his wife and children. For this he was taken to France where he walked through the gates of hell.

Part Two

This is the continuing story of Jesse and Amelia Warren now living in Walthamstow, East London from the end of the Great War which against all odds he survived, until their deaths many years later....but firstly it takes the reader back to the meeting of a young couple who were to survive many hardships. It tells of their family, the good times they shared together and the bad times but also it tells of many hilarious moments that will certainly make the reader smile.

Mill and Jesse Warren c.1911

GRATTON HOUSES,
GLOBE ROAD
BETHNAL GREEN,
EAST LONDON.

He took the King's Shilling
FOR THE LOVE OF AMELIA

It was Tuesday 15th February 1915. Jesse Warren, a young man of twenty-four years, stepped out from the main entrance of Gratton Houses, the East End dwellings where he lived with his wife Amelia and their two young daughters at Globe Road, Bethnal Green, East London. It was bitterly cold and Jesse felt a shiver as he stepped onto the pavement. The wind was beginning to blow and a sudden flurry of snow hit his face. He stood for a moment in hesitation, he had slept very little the night before and by the time morning had eventually arrived he had made his decision.

It wasn't a choice he had been eager to make, although it had been in the back of his mind as a possibility for the last two or three weeks. Jesse knew in his heart that the decision he had reached was really the only option open to him. He was not looking forward to the interview that lay ahead or the consequences that would no doubt follow but he knew there was no other way. Maybe if he were on his own it would be different for he could fend for himself. Heaven knows he'd managed that before but now with a wife and youngsters to support it was certainly a different kettle of fish. There was no way they could carry on living as they were and Jesse felt very disillusioned. This wasn't the life he'd planned for his family and until Britain had entered the war against Germany they'd been doing pretty well but life was certainly different now. He knew there was only one thing he could do to make sure Mill, (no one ever called her by her true name of Amelia) had a regular income to keep the girls and herself going until this blessed war was over.

Still hesitant Jesse looked about him, everything appeared to be grey and dirty, the windows of the small terraced houses opposite, the corner shop and even the lace curtains his neighbours were usually so particular about looked dingy. But this was London, as it always was and always would be in winter, so why should it be any different today?

It had all looked so familiar but standing there, his back to the building he had just left, Jesse was now seeing these surroundings in a different light as if perhaps for the first time. It was as if he had wanted to preserve the scene, to be remembered, just as it was that day.

Smoke that constantly bellowed from the hundreds, if not thousands, of neighbourhood chimneys had already discoloured the previous days snow transforming the stark whiteness into a thick black sludge. Although it was now getting on for 10 o'clock, the morning was still very dull and murky; the whole City of London was under a heavy blanket of dense fog caused by the colossal amount of coal fires that were constantly burning in household grates. Even those poor souls who were destitute and could no longer afford to buy coal would scrounge around for anything that would burn, broken discarded furniture, old boots and some, in sheer desperation to keep their children warm, had even taken up the odd floorboard.

Added to this was even more pollution, this came from the black smoke, smuts and soot that belched from the funnels of the railway trains as they ran in and out of the City. Along with the exhaust fumes from the ever-increasing number of vehicles that were now appearing on the streets it was no wonder that whatever the season, London was always known as 'The Smoke' and on a day like this, it was easy to see why. These treacherous London winters were also killers, deadly to the young and old alike. Influenza was spreading like wildfire and hundreds were now no doubt suffering from bronchitis and chest complaints caused by the damp and dense atmosphere. Many, if not taken already, would be dead before the spring and undertakers were always kept busy during these months. No one gave much thought to the appalling conditions winter always brought with it to London, that's how life in the 'Smoke' was and there was very little if anything that could be done to change it. It was an accepted way of life.

Globe Road, a turning off Old Ford Road to Jesse's left, was a rather long street curving slightly where the road was divided by Roman Road and the far end of Globe Road came out into the Mile End Road, nearing the Stepney area.

Coming slowly towards Jesse and taking up most of the road was the coal man. His load was being pulled by two massive shire horses both shaking their heads and tossing their manes while stamping their great hoofed feet in the wet sludge as if in protest of being led out from the comfort of the warm stables. The hot breath from their flaring nostrils turned into a vaporised fog around their heads.

"Coals!... coals!......, coals for cash only!" the man sitting next to the driver cried out.

"An' we ain't comin' back when the ol' man's out either, it's cash only!" The coal man and his mate were both shouting saucy remarks from their seats high up on the cart, letting customers know they were there. Despite the miserable and depressing weather like true cockneys they still showed their sense of humour.

As the driver came up to where Jesse was still standing he tugged on the reins bringing the two enormous animals to a halt.

Jesse being only a small man, slightly over 5' in height felt even smaller when the horses stopped just in front of where he stood.

"Coals for cash!" the driver called out again. "Coals for cash only!"

"You'll be bloody lucky round 'ere mate, no-one's got sod all!" Jesse called back.

"Well, those that wan'nit 'ad betta get in a bit sharpish", came the swift reply, "Ain't much left up the yard an' I ain't comin' back. It's all goin' to the bloody war ef'ert, might as well join up me self an' take me blooming 'orses with me!"

Jesse wondered if the shortage of fuel was really true or just a bit of scare mongering. It was bad enough going hungry but being without a fire as well would just about finish them all off. It was all right for those that had a job with a regular income because they didn't want for much; he'd learnt this as a fact of life years ago when he was just a lad.

The man had climbed down from his high seat; everything on him was covered in coal dust. He wore so many different jackets and jerkins that it was hard to say exactly what he did have on. On his head was a large cap worn back to front so as the peak was the wrong way round and a grubby scarf was knotted around his neck. A great leather yoke covered his huge shoulders, giving him protection from the tons of coal he humped all day by the sack full.

"Yeah, I reck'n you're right mate" he said, looking towards Jesse who was by the side of the cart, "should 'ave got well rid of this load by now"

A couple of doors opposite had opened as did a few windows in Gratton Houses behind.

"Git down ere' Bert an' see 'ow much the ol'e dear up there wants" he said giving instructions to the younger man, probably his son, who was still up in the seat. "I'll do the 'ouses and you can do the buildings", he added and began to pull one of the heavy hundredweight sacks from the cart onto his back.

Two small scruffy boys had been trailing behind the cart hoping to pick up any odd lumps of coal that might fall off to take back home to their mothers' or more than likely waiting for an opportunity to see what they could pinch while the two men weren't looking.

'Poor little blighter's' Jesse thought to himself knowing that many families were now in the same situation as him and Mill, stony broke and skint.

He put his hand inside the pocket of his overcoat to re-assure himself that he had the documents he would need, pulled his cloth cap down further over his head and turned up his collar. After covering his mouth and nose with the woollen muffler Mill had knitted as a protection from the cold and polluted air, he thrust his hands into his pockets and took a deep breath.

'Right then,' he mumbled gritting his teeth, 'this is it, no point standing 'ere all day'.

He then made his way left along Globe Road and turned into Old Ford Road passing the Greyhound Public House on the corner where he had spent many a happy hour with his mates, especially John Samuels one of his neighbours.

'Bloody war', he thought wishing he could go in for a jug. Several of his drinking mates had signed on in the last couple of months; even John had volunteered and had been posted to a Devonshire Regiment.

John Samuels and his wife Hetty were pals of Jesse and Mill's who lived next door but one to them in the buildings.

'I'd better see if she's heard anything from him when I get back' he thought to himself.

He had reached Cambridge Heath Road passing the newly built museum on his left. Being careful not to tread in the steaming dung left by a weary old mare that was pulling an uncovered cart, he crossed the main road. The cart was loaded with furniture that had long since seen better days. A woman wrapped in a blanket sat in the back with two small children; no doubt it was her ol' man up front. Jesse knew this was a sign of yet another hard up family been evicted and goodness knows where they were heading. He didn't need reminding that his own rent was now well overdue and Mill was living in dread of being served with the eviction notice which they both knew would soon be inevitable.

"It will be over my dead body before I'll let that happen to my lot" he muttered and with determination quickened his step, feeling uneasy at his own thoughts.

He turned into Three Colts Lane where Mill's family had once lived, his boots made a squelching sound in the wet slush underfoot. It was only about a mile and half to his destination, but already he could feel the damp seeping through the hole he thought he'd made good the night before with a piece of cardboard.

Jesse Warren knew this side of the Thames like the back of his hand; he'd been born just the same as Mill in Hoxton Old Town near Shoreditch, just a couple of miles walk from Bethnal Green. Although unlike Mill whose family had moved to Walthamstow when she was a youngster, he had lived around these parts all his life. It was Shoreditch he was now heading back to, desperately wishing it were under different circumstances.

Back in Gratton Houses at number 122, Mill was beginning to wonder where Jesse had gone to this time. She hoped that he would have some luck in finding a few days work, goodness knows he had tried hard enough. He'd been gone some time now and she was beginning to worry. Maybe he's got a job and had started already she thought trying to convince herself as she poked at the few burning coals in the kitchen range, the white ash falling into the pan below. Not so long ago she had been cooking all their meals on it but there was nothing to cook now.

There was just enough coal left in the coal 'ole out on the landing to last a few more days. So long as the girls were warm she and Jesse could cope but when the last of the coal had gone well, she just didn't know what they would do or how on earth they would manage.

Not that long ago the coal man had left a couple of hundredweight sacks each week, he'd even let her have a sack or two on tick when things started getting bad but now she knew it would be useless to ask for more credit. Lord knows they were desperate for money and hearing the coal men shouting outside didn't do much to lift her spirits. Mill knew only too well that they were now deep in what she and other East Enders could only describe as being in 'Shite' Street.

To save on fuel they were living and sleeping in the one room. It was a comfortable room, although rather overcrowded now that their own bed and the cot for the eldest daughter Elizabeth was in there too.

The upper half of the walls above the chair rail was papered with large pink roses and twisted vines. The lower half Jesse had painted deep cream over the thick lincrusta paper. When they had first moved in all the woodwork in the room, including the bottom half of the walls had been dark green. Mill always hated anything green, she always thought of it as being unlucky although she never said why. So Jesse had changed the colour for her with a quick coat of cream paint.

The wooden floor was covered in well worn brown linoleum. A rag rug lay in front of the kitchen range where the low fire was burning. The wooden clothes horse that Jesse had made stood nearby covered with nappies and damp clothes. Opposite was the door that led out onto the communal landing and stairs.

The recesses either side of the kitchen range were fitted with low wooden cupboards. Two small fireside chairs sat in front

14

and above on the walls were gaslights. It had been some time since there had been any coppers to feed the meter so firelight and candles were now the only means of lighting. On the mantelpiece several half-burnt candles stood on saucers, each one held upright by the melted wax. A small wooden clock that Jesse had re-polished himself ticked away steadily. The cot for Elizabeth had been placed in front of the door on the right that had led into the bedroom that was no longer in use.

To the left was a long sash window with wine coloured curtains pulled back to the sides. The window itself was now bare and the glass was grubby on the outside from the smoke and grime of London. Condensation was beginning to form on the inside from the damp washing and snow that had since turned to black sludge had settled on the outside window ledge and along the bottom of the window. Not so long ago there had been a heavy cream lace curtain hanging there but like many of their other possessions, had since gone. Mill and Jesse were terrified of being evicted and had gradually sold anything they had of value to raise money for the rent. They were in such a dire situation that it had meant going short on food and bare necessaries as long as the rent was paid on time and they had a roof over their heads. Now they had nothing and the rent man would soon be knocking for money they hadn't got. All they had left now were just the essential everyday items and apart from the clock, little if anything left to sell.

Elizabeth who was two years old (although always known in the family as 'young' Milly) was sitting on the big brass bed that had come from the now unused bedroom happily playing with a rag doll. Even the lovely white candlewick bedspread Mill had bought just before they married had since been sold for a pittance.

Beatrice, (Cissy to the family) their three-month-old baby slept contentedly in a wicker basket that rested on two chairs facing each other.

Things couldn't get any worst and Mill was dreading the thought of having to go and queue at the soup kitchen in nearby Old Ford Road where the unfortunate down and outs of Bethnal Green gathered on a daily basis. The shame of having to do that and the humiliation of waiting in a queue for a bowl of soup was something she just could not face.

If it weren't for Billy, the son of her friend and neighbour Mrs Johnson who lived upstairs they would have to resort to the soup kitchen which was Mill's worst nightmare, to think they had to come that... if it hadn't been for Billy they wouldn't be eating today. The kindly lad had a job in the kitchens of a hotel somewhere up the West End and any scraps left on customers' plates or stale bread from the kitchens would go into a bag which he would then bring home and give to Mill. Somehow he always managed to include a tin of evaporated milk,

'For the kiddies' he would say,

Mill was sure he was buying the milk himself but whenever she had asked, he would just smile and touch his nose. A way of saying, 'Never you mind!'

Thankfully, he had kept them going for the last week or two by bringing the scraps whenever he could and no doubt by having a job did his best to help out his parents. His father was unable to work through chronic bronchitis although his mother did earn a bit of money by delivering babies and laying out the dead but it was well known that she preferred to spend her earnings on gin. Mill and Jesse would never ever forget the kindness of Billy and would always be indebted to him for a long as they lived.

Being the eldest of fourteen children, Mill knew how to make the best out of whatever they were given, but it was degrading for them to be eating other people's leftovers.

Scraps of food that were intended for the pigs bin and dry crusts were now being soaked in gravy to feed a family. Jesse hated it,

"We're even doing the bloody pigs out of their grub!" he had shouted as he left earlier that morning, not saying where he was going.

They had moved into Gratton Houses which was a comparatively new building compared with the many old Victorian tenements in the district. Gratton Houses had been built by the east End Dwelling Company and had housed many families who could afford the rent.

Being a French polisher by trade Jesse hadn't wanted for work when they first moved there and Mill had also found herself employment as a machinist in a nearby shirt factory so the young couple were doing pretty well for themselves. They could pay their rent on time, buy coal and put pennies in the gas meter for their lighting. Mill was also able to buy good food and they ate well and there was always enough left for a couple of drinks in the nearby Greyhound Public House on a Saturday night

She had worked at the factory until four weeks before her first child was born. It was Billy's mother, Mrs Johnson who had the self appointed job of not only laying out the deceased but also being the local mid-wife and it was her who delivered young Milly in the January of 1913. She'd had no training for delivering babies or for laying out the dead, that was considered 'women's work' but whenever a birth was imminent or someone had breathed their last; it was Mrs Johnson who they would send for. Her fee was always the same; whether she was laying out some poor soul who had recently departed from this life or bringing a new one into it her fee was always the same, "*Just a couple of pennies or a drop of gin will do dear*" she would say to a new mother or a bereaved relative and they would be very happy to pay her, in one way or the other.

With the birth of young Milly came the very first maternity grants. Mill had paid her contributions while at work and two days after her baby was born she was one of the very first women to receive a Government Maternity Grant of 30/- (£1.50p), which was a 'Godsend' for all new mothers, and especially those who already had several other children to feed. Unfortunately in some cases the money was spent in the public houses and not as David Lloyd George, the Chancellor of Exchequer who had campaigned for these benefits had intended.

Six months later Mill went back to work in the shirt factory leaving young Milly in the care of Hetty Samuels, Jesse's mates wife who lived two doors along their landing at 126. Mrs Johnson had offered but Mill tactfully told her it might be difficult if she was called out on a job. Truth was that Mill wasn't too keen to leave young Milly with her just in case she'd had a 'laying out' the night before or a confinement and had been on the gin. Jesse hadn't wanted Mill to go back to work but things were beginning to get a bit slack for him and he wasn't getting as much work as before. Mill suggested she'd just do it until things picked up again so he'd agreed, hoping she was right.

However, lately there had been a lot of talk and rumours of a forth-coming war and the machinists were now making uniforms by the thousands in case the worst came to the worst and the ordinary man in the street was called upon to volunteer. She was soon helping to produce protective masks in case deadly poison gases were used on the troops. These consisted of a heavy white linen hood that covered the head and face. Something resembling goggles covered the holes cut for the eyes and a mouthpiece had a breathing tube of sorts attached. Mill's job was to machine the seams together and as she did so she often prayed that no man would ever use such a wicked poison gas against another human being.

Thankfully at the time, as she said these prayers she and millions of other women, mothers, sisters, wives and sweethearts throughout the country had no idea then of the horrors that would come within such a short time and just how many of their men folk would go to war and never return.

Then, to everyone's shock and disbelief war against Germany was finally declared in August 1914.

Soon young women who'd expected to spend the rest of their lives in Service had a new-found freedom by working with fair pay and shorter hours in the factories.

Uniforms were now needed by the thousands, ammunition factories were in full swing and posters of Lord Kitchener the Secretary of War were being stuck up everywhere with him pointing a finger under the caption;

'Your Country Needs... You!'

In the December of 1914 Mill gave birth to their second daughter, Beatrice (Cissy to the family).

By then Jesse had no work what so-ever. Since war had been declared and with so many men now away fighting in France, the last thing people wanted was their furniture re-polished. Mill had used the maternity grant she'd received when Cissy was born to keep them going for a short time and had even applied to get her old machining job back which she had given up when she was several months pregnant but there were just no vacancies, the factories were full. Women were even queuing with the hope of not only getting employment where they would be independent for the first time in their lives but to do their bit for the country and war effort.

Hundreds of men were volunteering every day and soon women would be working on the trams, railways and other jobs which would never had been expected of them before.

Even some of the shops in the area were shutting up. Many had painted, 'Closed for the duration' across their shutters. Several, being optimistic had added, 'Reopen in 6 months'.

Things were really bad by now, the war had already been going on for six month even though many had said and thought it would be over by Christmas. However, Christmas had come and gone and it was now mid February.

Lord Kitchener was still encouraging the ordinary man in the streets to join the Army and help with winning the war. The price of food was rising rapidly and Jesse had been trying for days to find work and was willing to take on any kind of employment but there was just nothing to be had. Employers could see no point in taking on a young man like Jesse knowing that in all probability he'd soon be giving his notice to go and join up. No, women were the only ones being given work and they were now doing jobs that had once been a man's work. The world was certainly changing.

With no money to pay their rents, people were being evicted from their homes. It was always the same, if you didn't pay your rent you were out; it was as simple as that. As a very last resort there was always the dreaded Workhouse but most people would rather sleep in doorways and beg on the streets than go there. In fact that's what many did. It was only when sickness and deep despair took over that they had no other choice.

Jesse had known starvation only too well as a child and was not having his children living the way he'd had to. His own mother Mary Ann had died after giving birth to two children within ten months. She had gone into premature labour on the very same day his 10-month-old sister Lily had died from bronchitis and convulsions. Lily's frail little body had lain in a wooden draw waiting for the undertaker to take her away while Mary Ann bled to death from a haemorrhage that lasted five days, during which time the new-born baby had also succumbed. Mary Ann had been just twenty-seven years old when she died in 1897. Jesse himself was only seven at the time and had vague memories of other babies being born to his mother, only to die shortly afterwards.

His younger sister Annie and he were the only two who survived.

Their father was not able, or more than likely did not want to cope with this sorry state of affairs. After seeing his wife and two children buried together in the same coffin, he left his daughter Annie in the care of an old family friend known to everyone as Granny Clarke, abandoned Jesse to look after himself and made off with another woman.

When things got really bad Jesse did sometimes stay with Aunt Amy, his mother's sister. She did her best for him but having a large family herself was struggling to make ends meet and Jesse was soon off roughing it on the streets of London like many other children of that era. Living off his wits, sleeping in any shelter he could find, out in all weathers and knowing only too well the pangs of hunger and cold. He learnt at a very early age how to look after himself and to do so in more ways than one. He learnt how to run; and to run fast, especially when a bobby's whistle was blowing behind him!

By the time he was in his teens he knew how to use his fists and how to use a convenient piece of timber that may have been lying around as a weapon of self- defence. He was always quick to give anyone who was being set upon a helping hand when needed. One such occasion had landed him in the local nick for seven days when he was just seventeen but not before the hospital had first put several stitches in his head. Another time when Jesse was 'lending a hand' he received a deep cut above the right eye and despite his height or lack of it, he was soon known in the area as a tough street fighter. He had to be if he wanted to survive in those back streets and alleyways of East London.

He'd even earned a couple of bob once when he pulled a dead body out from the Thames. He'd learnt to swim in a local canal as a young lad and was a good strong swimmer. On this occasion he was crossing London Bridge when he saw several people looking down into the river. Out of curiosity he went to see what was going on and saw a body which appeared to be that of a woman floating face down in the water. A crowd had gathered along the embankment and a local copper was standing near the edge with a long stick trying to pull the body in. Jesse hurried down the steps that led to the water's edge, pulled off his boots and dived in. The body was now out of reach of the copper's stick but with a few strong strokes he soon reached the poor unfortunate woman. He grabbed hold of her coat and swam pulling her back to where the onlookers were standing. A round of applause went up and a few shouts of "Well done lad, well done!"

The copper took over proceedings and not only thanked Jesse but gave him two shillings (10p).

It wasn't unusual around this time for a corpse to be found floating in the Thames. Some may have fallen in, maybe missing their footing when staggering home late at night stone drunk, some may have been pushed in after foul play had taken place but sadly many young women met their deaths this way, especially when they were unmarried, pregnant and destitute.

Aunt Amy did try to see that Jesse got some education when he had turned up occasionally and most likely sent him to school with her own children because he did learn to read and write. By the time he was fourteen he had a job selling lemons in a nearby market and eventually did move in with

Aunt Amy. One day he happened to be passing a shop in Cambridge Heath Road that sold furniture when he noticed in the window a card which read, *Lad wanted for general duties.* He went inside and the first thing that hit him was the smell. He was later to learn that this smell was cellulose which was used when giving furniture that wonderful high gloss finish which was known as French Polish.

Jesse got the job and began by sweeping up and running errands for the owner and he did very well for himself for as time passed he learnt the trade and became a very skilful French Polisher.

When he left to get married in 1911 Aunt Amy gave him two mementos to keep; a lock of his mother's hair taken as she lay in her coffin and the receipt for the costs of burying her and his two little sisters. Jesse never did know whether his father had intentionally left them for him or whether he had just carelessly left them behind.

However they were the only things he ever had to remind him of his mother and he cherished them to his dying day.

It was during 1910, when working on a special commission for a gent living in Walthamstow that he'd met Mill. She was two years older than him being born in the July of 1888. Jesse had been born in the July of 1890. They became engaged but waited until Christmas Day 1911 to marry. The ceremony took place in Mill's local Parish Church, St. James the Greater, at the junction of Markhouse Road and St. James's Street.

Now it was 1915 and life had taken a turn for the worst again, but no way was Jesse Frederick Warren going to stand by and see his wife and children suffer the way he had. There was only one thing left that he could do to end this misery and suffering and he had done it, there was no turning back.

Mill looked at the clock on the mantelpiece, it was just on 3.30 in the afternoon and already it was nearly dark outside. Jesse still hadn't returned and she was about to look out of the window before drawing the curtains when suddenly the door of their apartment flew open and in he walked carrying a large brown bag. His face was flushed, not only from the cold outside but also from the day's events. Before Mill could say anything Jesse came out with the words she had never ever wanted to hear and she felt her heart turn to ice. "I've joined up" he said, "I've taken the King's Shilling"

Hetty Samuels, friend of Mill and Jesse, with her son John and his wife. Taken in later life c.1950's.

Chapter Two

The idea of an ordinary working class chap like himself being accepted as a soldier for the Army made Jesse very apprehensive. In his time he'd been in street fights where occasionally broken bottles had been brandished about but he'd never been threatened by anyone possessing firearms.

'I wouldn't even know how to load a bloody rifle, let alone fire one' he thought as he approached the Army Recruiting Office at Shoreditch that morning.

Although now a family man, Jesse hadn't lost his reputation for being a bit of a bruiser. He could still hand out a bashing when it came to a good punch up, which invariably happened on Saturday nights after the pubs had closed. Those Saturday nights wouldn't have been the same in the East End if a disturbance hadn't taken place somewhere in the neighbourhood and Bethnal Green was no exception.

Jesse along with his mate John Samuels had often found themselves involved in a disagreement of some sort usually while supping a few beers in one of the local pubs. More often than not, these disputes started inside the nearby 'Greyhound' on the corner where they both lived. The offer of getting it 'sorted outside' at closing time was always considered the best method for settling any argument and a crowd always gathered to spur them on. Then by the time it was all over no one could remember what had started it all off in the first place!

However, fighting in the Army would certainly be different to a Saturday night brawl on the pavement in front of the local pub. At least there they shook hands afterwards and called out,' See yer tomorrow mate!' before stumbling home, usually singing drunkenly as they went on their way, more often than not nursing a black eye and a few bruises. There'd be none of that if he did end up in France.

Lack of height had never stopped Jesse getting involved in any wrangle or brawl, he just waded in. Being short and slightly built may not have held him back, but it certainly didn't give him the appearance of the Military type either. He just didn't look like the sort who would be accepted by the Army, for a start being only 5'2" maybe he wasn't tall enough.......

This thought hadn't crossed his mind before and caused him to stop dead in his tracks, 'Blimey, supposing they say I'm not tall enough and won't accept me?'

He was suddenly horrified that he might get turned down and yet at the same time, just as horrified if they accepted him.

Jesse couldn't miss the old church hall that had been a Working Man's Club for the last few years, although now taken over by the Army. Apart from posters stuck all over the outside walls proclaiming that men were needed for what they now referred to as, 'Kitchener's New Army', a large sign had been erected over the entrance which read;

Army Recruiting Office
All Branches of the Army
Apply Within

 Two burly khaki uniformed soldiers were standing either side of the entrance. Both were a good six-foot tall and wore peaked caps and heavy great coats.

On seeing the soldiers, Jesse's first instinct was to turn around and head back to Bethnal Green! However, the thought of Mill and the girls' waiting at home gave him the courage he now desperately needed. In his heart he knew they couldn't continue living the way they were. This was the only chance he would have to see them all right.

Army pay wasn't brilliant, but at least it would buy food and see them through until it was all over and life in the East End was back to normal. Hopefully that wouldn't be too long now. There was talk of the British and French Governments planning a big push to drive the Germans back out of Belgium finishing the war once and for all.

This they said, would be the War to end all Wars, so it couldn't last much longer once the German's had been given the big 'heave-ho'. Everyone had been talking about it and Jesse reasoned that by the time he had done his basic training the war would have more than likely finished any way. If this turned out the way they were led to believe then he may not even have to go to France after all. Thousands of men had volunteered to give the Regulars a hand and so far the Government hadn't brought in Conscription.

Jesse therefore had high hopes of the War coming to a swift end once this big push started. Enlisting only meant that you were there if needed. Jesse wasn't doing that, he was actually joining up. He had to if he wanted a regular income for Mill and the girls and it was the only way to give them a better existence. He felt sick to think of what they had since been reduced to and the way they were now struggling to survive.

Several men were going into the Recruiting Office and Jesse followed. His left foot felt painfully numb from the icy cold slush that had by now penetrated the sodden cardboard. He walked towards the entrance, wishing he could go home instead.

The two soldiers standing either side of the doorway, both towering above Jesse, touched their caps as he walked past, "Morning Sir" said one of them.

"Blimey!" Jesse thought, not being used to such courtesy, 'who the hell do they think I am, bloody Lord Kitchener himself?'

'Morning,' he muttered in return, given the soldier a hasty glance.

Jesse found himself in a small flag stoned entrance room. He loosened his now wet muffler and removed his damp cap.

The floor was wet from the sludge brought in on the men's boots. On his right next to each other were two doors, one marked, *'Ladies Powder Room'* and the other *'Gents Urinals.'* The smell of carbolic, stale tobacco and urine reached his nostrils. A door to his left had a sign which said *'Kitchen'*. Jesse hadn't eaten since the bit of piecrust Mill had soaked in a weak gravy the night before. Even the word kitchen made him realise just how hungry he was.

In front of him was a pair of swing doors, the upper halves having frosted glass. The men who he'd seen entering the Hall from outside had already gone through. Jesse stood for a moment feeling unsure, his confidence momentary leaving him. Suddenly one of the doors opened and two chaps walk out, both about the same age as him.

"Good luck mate!" the first one said when he saw Jesse standing there.

"Yeah", said the second man, holding the door open for him, "See yer in the Mutton Lancers!"

"Ta", replied Jesse as he walked into the hall, not having the faintest idea what the chap was on about.

Now inside there was no going back, Jesse looked around. The first thing he noticed was a large desk set lengthways bang in the middle of the somewhat dimly lit small hall. Behind the desk sat another army bloke, taking notes. A queue with just a dozen or so stood to one side, Jesse walked across to join them. It wasn't exactly hot in there, but it was a damn sight warmer inside than out. He wished he could take his boots off and give his feet a good rub.

About fifty or so men were sitting around in small groups or just on their own while some stood with their backs leaning against the walls having a smoke. Jesse noticed others retrieving chairs from a folded pile stacked near a raised platform at one end of the hall to his left.

"Next!" the soldier called out from behind the desk and the queue moved up a couple of paces.

Along the wall to the back of the desk were a row of small dingy windows, like the hall itself, in need of a good clean. The paint on the walls had a trace of once being cream, although now grubby and badly marked. It had been many years since they'd seen a decent coat of paint. Several men were puffing on pipes or smoking roll ups and tobacco smoke hung heavy in the air. Overhead a couple of hissing gaslights were sending out a dull yellow glow that mingled with the smoky atmosphere.

At the opposite end of the hall from the raised platform, which had probably served as a stage at one time were several screens similar to those used in hospitals.

Jesse heard a name being called and watched as a man got up from his seat and followed a soldier. The area partitioned off by means of the screens was obviously where the recruits were being interviewed. Some men sat with clasped hands resting on their knees, heads bowed looking at the floor. Others were talking in low voices having a quiet confab together.

He recognised one chap as the butcher from Cambridge Heath Road near to where he lived, not that Mill ever went in his shop any more.

Christ Almighty, Jesse muttered to himself as he recalled the lovely lamb stews she used to make let alone a nice bit of beef on a Sunday. He noticed that the butcher was still wearing his striped apron and straw hat.

Don't know what he wants to sign up for, aint because he's got no grub on the table

"Next!" called the soldier from behind the desk and the queue moved up again

Jesse felt a light tap on his shoulder and an extremely snooty voice from behind began,

"Oh… I say my good fellow, rather quick that soldier chappie is…. don't you think?"

Turning he found an older man, possibly in his mid thirties standing there dressed in a pinstriped morning suit and wearing a black bowler. He had an umbrella hanging on one arm and a camel hair coat with red satin lining draped over the other. Jesse was just about eye level to a red silk cravat that sported a diamond pin.

"Yeah, I fink they're jus' takin' names first mate." he replied, wondering what on earth a bloke like that was doing there.

The gent looked at his watch. Jesse was quick to spot the genuine thing.

'Blimey!' he thought, that ain't yer every day brass he's got there, its blooming gold. The real McCoy! He must be worth a few bob.'

"I do hope I'm not kept too long, I have a very important appointment at two-thirty this after -noon" the gent was telling Jesse, who wasn't partially interested in this bloke's afternoon arrangements,

"Well, wot yer doin' 'er then?" he asked sarcastically in his cockney accent.

"One has to do one's bit, you know my dear chap. Always willing to give the young boys a hand" he replied as he removed his kid gloves, Jesse noticed the gold cuff links the gent wore.

Jesse had no patience for this sort. Here was some Toff, loaded with money who probably had never even heard of the word hunger, flashing a gold watch and cuff links in front of him and he was just about to suggest to the Toff that he should sod off when the soldier behind the desk called,

"Next!" and the queue moved along.

Jesse decided it would be better to ignore this toffee nosed gent, but the man had other ideas.

Referring to the soldier sitting behind the desk, he said,

"Nice boy isn't he? I do like to see them in uniform... does something for a young man, don't you agree?"

The penny dropped, Jesse clenched his fists ready to give a bunch of fives, but restrained himself. This was the last place he wanted to start a fight.

"I'd piss off if I were you mate", Jesse said turning to face him, "I don't think they want yer sort in 'ere"

"Next!"

The queue moved up, there was just a young lad in front of Jesse.

"How old are you sonny?" the soldier asked. Jesse couldn't help overhearing.

The lad was a bit hesitant,

"Err... nineteen Sir," he stammered, obviously lying.

"What year were you born in then?"

This threw the lad a bit and he mumbled "Err...1899 Sir"

"What year are we in now then?"

Jesse knew the soldier was trying to catch the lad out.

"1915" replied the lad,

"Well if I were you sonny, I'd go off for a walk and come back this afternoon, you might have been born in 1896 by then"

"Yes Sir". The young lad getting the gist of what was being implied turned and walked towards the door.

'Christ!' Jesse thought, 'he's only a bloody kid'

"Next!" It was now Jesse's turn. He noticed from the two stripes the soldier wore on his arm that he was a Corporal. Not that he knew much about army ranks but he'd seen a bloke wearing army uniform one night in the Greyhound with two stripes and overheard him being called Corporal.

"Name?"

"Warren.....Sir", he answered trying to make a good impression.

The Corporal started taking notes.

 "First names?"

"Jesse Frederick, Sir".

"Age?"

"Twenty Four, Sir", the soldier looked up at Jesse, convinced he was giving his true age, carried on with his questions,

"Married?"

"Yes Sir"

"Got your marriage certificate?"

"Yes Sir,"

"Children?"

"Yes Sir, two"

"Got their birth certificates with you?"

Jesse had sneaked these from the cupboard drawer without Mill knowing.

"Yes Sir"

"Right then Warren" "get your-self a chair and wait to be called," then as an after thought added, "There'll be a cup of tea over there in a minute" and nodded towards a large shuttered counter, probably used as a bar before the Army took the place over.

 "There's no charge, it's on the Army. Next!"

Jesse couldn't believe his luck. Hot tea! That would be welcome more than a jug of ale. He put his cap in his pocket and made his way towards a recently vacated chair.

 Just as he was passing, the shutters over the counter went up. There was a sudden scurry as men jumped from their seats and hurried towards him.

Always being quick of the mark Jesse thought, 'Sod this, I'm getting in now!' and somehow found him-self first in the queue.

Women were working behind the counter, obviously the kitchen that led from the entrance hall. One of the women handed Jesse a large mug of steaming tea, "There's sugar in that one dearie, that alright?" she asked.

"Cor, fanks luv," Jesse said as he gratefully took the hot drink, "you may not believe it, but I reckon you've saved me life".

The woman smiled, "Well here you are then ducks, might as well have one of these to go with it then" she passed Jesse a large flat Arrowroot biscuit, "first come, first served, ain't many left".

Jesse nearly cried, someone had given him a biscuit. With two kiddies and a wife at home desperately short of food, he felt very beholden.

It was of course very tempting to dunk the biscuit in his tea and eat it there and then. Lord knows he was hungry enough, but he thought of the girls and put the biscuit in his overcoat pocket.

'If they accept me, then I'll eat it', Jesse thought to himself, "if not I'll take it home'.

All being well and he was accepted, there would be the 2/10d (14p) Attestation fee.   With that he could buy some desperately needed food to take back home.

Moving away from the queue that had soon formed behind, he stood for a while drinking the sweet tea, both hands cradling the mug. A hot drink like that was Heaven; perhaps joining the Army wasn't such a bad idea after all!

There were plenty of empty chairs now, some men had already been seen to but had waited to get a free cup of tea and a biscuit. Not wanting to pinch anyone's seat that may be getting tea, Jesse pulled a chair from the stack by the stage. He held the mug in one hand while he flicked the folded chair open with the other being careful not to spill the tea. He put the mug down on the seat while he removed his muffler and overcoat and laid them over the back. Then picking up the mug sat down to await his name being called.

He sat watching the proceedings. There was a queue right through the swing doors which had since been bolted back against the walls; he was pleased that he had got there when he had. Every ten minutes or so another soldier collected notes from the desk in the middle of the hall and took them back behind the screens.

Jesse was thinking about taking his boots off to give his feet a rub. His toes were giving him gyp with the cold and by now one boot had been squelching as he walked but thought better of it. He would probably have to take them off soon anyway when he was called for the medical.

"All right if I sit 'ere mate?" asked a bloke who had brought a chair over to where Jesse was sitting.

"Yeah, 'elp yourself".

The man was dressed like most of them in the hall, a heavy worn overcoat that had seen better days, a knotted scarf and cloth cap.

"Been 'er long?

"'Bout an hour or so I reckon", replied Jesse.

"Watch me seat would yer mate, while I'll get a cuppa. Wan'na refill while I'm there?" Jesse thought he seemed a decent type, a real Londoner like himself and jumped at the chance of another mug of tea. .

"Ere give us yer mug then" and off he went to join the queue at the counter,

Jesse wondered if there would be another biscuit but when the fellow returned about five minutes later he only had tea. Jesse was grateful for a chance of a second mug.

The two men began talking.

"How long you signing on for then?" Jesse's companion wanted to know, "Doing the Duration?"

Yeah" answered Jesse, "That will long enough for me. Just the short service. He certainly had no intentions of making a career out of the Army.

"Name's Bert, by the way" he said introducing himself.

"Pleased to meet yer mate, name's Jesse Warren", the men shook hands.

Bert went on to say that he couldn't wait to join up which surprised Jesse.

"Do anything to get away from me ol' woman" he said, "She's only been and let her ol' mother come and stay at our place, the naggin' ol' cow. Right ol' battleaxe she is". He paused for a moment, "Not only that, she's only bin and brought 'er six grown up kids with 'er an' all. I've already got eight kids of me own living in the same 'ouse, all bloody women, the whole lot of them! Like the loony bin it is back there. They don't stop screaming and shouting at each other all day an' night an' what with 'em leaving their wet drawers an' 'fings hanging around everywhere, I've 'ad enough, I'm getting out of it."

Bert still hadn't finished telling Jesse his problems,

"I even 'ad a bloody hat pin stick in me arse the other night, one of the silly cows only left 'er 'at in me best armchair. Then she only 'ad a go at me 'cos I'd squashed the bloody thing, nah, I'd rather join the Army an' get away from the ol'e bloody lot of 'em."

Jesse laughed, "Yeah, I don't blame yer mate, think I'd do the same if I was you!"

"Some of 'em 'ave only bin down me depot" Bert went on, "and put their names down for jobs. Bad enough 'aving to live with 'em, let alone 'aving 'em work with me an' all "

Jesse asked him what he did for a living,

"Work on the trams mate, 'ave done for years. But now they're only going to take on women. They reckon it ain't worth taking on men, case they all join up. Ain't worth training 'em, see."

Jesse thought that was a pity, he wouldn't have minded having a go at that himself.

"Not only that", Bert went on, continuing his tale and feeling dissatisfied with the way things had turned out for him, "some 'ave even got themselves jobs in the munitions factories, can you imagine women doing that? Mind you, lots of 'em look like flipping canaries now 'cos of that TNT chemical they stuff the shells with, it's turning their skin bright yellow. Nah, I reckon I'll be better off in the Army".

Jesse told him how things were at home.

"My Missus doesn't even know I'm 'ere, she probably thinks I'm out looking for work. She'll go barmy when she knows I've joined up and she'll do 'er nut, but there ain't no other choice. There's no work going and we've got sod all. I've tried talking to 'er about it but she just won't listen."

"Don't think my ol' lady will even notice I've gone" Bert said as he brought a tin of baccy from of his coat pocket, "Fancy a roll up?

"Yeah, thanks mate, don't mind if I do." Jesse replied, even though he very rarely smoked.

He was beginning to feel a bit anxious now, knowing his name would be called soon. Maybe a fag would help calm him down a bit.

Suddenly there was a commotion in the middle of the hall. A woman was banging her fist on the desk. The two burly soldiers from outside had followed her in. She looked rather bedraggled as if she had been running "Where the bloody hell is he!" she shouted breathlessly, banging her fist on the desk again.

There was a sudden hush in the hall as everyone looked at the woman,

"Where's my boy?" she cried, "where is he?"

The Corporal at the desk jumped up rather startled, "Who are you looking for Madam?" he asked rather taken back.

"I'm looking for me son that's who, what ave 'yer done with 'em? And don't call me Madam!"

"What's his name Mad...errr Misses?"

"Sod his bloody name, he's only sixteen and he ain't joining up!" she screamed as she looked around the hall.

Suddenly she spotted her son, sitting down near the screens.

"Right!" she said as she marched over to where he was sitting and pulled the lad to his feet. If he was only sixteen, he certainly didn't look it. He was a big built lad, about 5' 10" tall.

"Git yer self out of 'ere, you daft bugger!" she shouted as she reached up and gave the boy a smack round the ear, much to the amusement of all the onlookers.

"They've already got yer ol' man an' yer two brothers so they ain't having you an' all! Now sod off home before I giv'yer another clout!"

"Look Misses", said the Corporal who had been taking the notes, "we have this man down as nineteen."

"Man my arse!" she said pushing the boy in front of her, "He's coming 'ome with me an' if yer don't like it, then it's bloody hard luck! Don't know what the world's comin' to, takin' flipping kids to do a man's work"

A group of about thirty lads had entered the hall and were gathered near the doorway.

"Go on Mother!, one called as all they stood aside to let her pass, "Take him home and tuck him in bed!".

"Mind yer own sodding business!" she shouted back, "You're all a load of daft buggers, why don't yer sod off 'ome to yer mother's where yer belong!"

A round of applause and laughter went around the hall as she pushed her now very embarrassed son out through the doors followed by the two soldiers who had followed in behind her.

"Well that certainly livened fings up," Bert said as he laughed.

"Yeah, you've to see the funny side of fings, ain't yeah?" Jesse couldn't help laughing himself.

The lads by the door were now fooling about, shoving and pushing at each other, trying to get in line. They were all dressed alike and were wearing long overcoats, straw boaters and blue and white striped woollen scarves around their necks. None of them could have been more than eighteen if that and looked as if they were from some posh Public School.

"Come on!" called one of them in a well educated voice, "Let's get over there and give the Jerries a shove!"

"Yes!" cried another lad, pretending to fire a machine gun. "Let's go and finish them off once and for all! Ratta tat, tat.... ratta tat tat!"

"They will soon run when they see your ugly face Hamilton!" one called back full of banter. "You won't need a gun!"

Another lad dressed the same as the others entered the hall "Come on Buckingham," they called to him, "where have you been? The war will be over by the time you get your name down!"

"Let's see some action!" whooped another.

"Right, Gentleman! Let's have a bit of order please!" said the Corporal showing some authority and the lads quietened down.

"Warren, Jesse Frederick!"

Jesse felt his stomach turn over as he heard his name being called,

"Well that's me then" he said to Bert as he stood up, collecting his coat and muffler from the back of the chair.

Bert stood up as well, "We'll 'ave to meet up for a drink when this is all over mate"

"Yeah," Jesse replied, "You'll probably find me in the Greyhound down the Old Ford Road most Saturday nights. Let's 'ope it ain't too long before it's all sorted out."

"Well, long as I get away from me ol' lady for a while" Bert joked, "I'll be 'appy!"

The two men laughed and shook hands and wished each other all the best.

"See yer around mate, thanks' for the smoke." Jesse put the remains of the fag that had since gone out into his pocket thinking he might want it later and headed towards the screens. '

Chapter Three

The first thing Jesse did when he walked out of the Recruiting Office was to eat the biscuit he'd been keeping in his overcoat pocket. The biscuit that he had been so tempted to eat was now his. He had earned the right to eat it. He was also tempted to light the fag end he still had but didn't have a match so he tossed it to some poor soul sitting in a doorway who gratefully accepted it.

No longer would he be known as Mr. Warren. He was now;

Pte. Jesse Frederick Warren 4727

Assigned to the

2nd. Battalion of the Queen's Royal West Surrey's.

Regiment

The Army had accepted him and he was now a soldier of the King. Jesse let out a sigh as he put his cap back on, relieved that the business of joining up was now over and done with and as he headed home he thought back over the last few hours.

After the long wait and then hearing his name being called there had been a quick medical examination. Apart from being slightly undernourished his health was fine.

"Well what else do you expect when you're living on sod all!" he'd nearly blurted out, but decided against it. So far everything had gone in his favour but it was the next bit of the proceedings he'd been concerned about: "Relax and breath normally" an Army doctor in a white coat had said as he'd put a tape measure around Jesse's chest.

"32 inches" he called to a Private who was taking notes.

"Breath in please Warren….. hold it. Right, breath out" the doctor told him looking at the tape measure,

"Expansion, 32.5 inches".

Jesse had dreaded the next bit. He'd stood against the measuring scale stretching himself to his maximal height and held his breath. The doctor slid the indicator down until it rested on his head.

"5 foot 1.5 inches….right, that's fine Warren", the doctor was happy with that and told Jesse to get dressed and then go along to a Sergeant Williams who was sitting at a nearby table.

Jesse was only too happy that his height hadn't let him down; he'd passed the medical with flying colours. The worst bit was putting a cold wet sock back on!

Next he was asked a load of questions and he'd been surprised at what they wanted to know, where and when Mill had been born, where they had married, Mill's full name and maiden name, how old she was plus all his own details. Mill of course he named as his Next of Kin. However, Jesse did remember to give her name as Amelia Charlotte Warren formerly Herod and not just Mill for all these official documents.

Information about the children was noted and Jesse handed over the certificates required as proof for the wife and children allowance.

After taking down all those necessary details required by law he was asked to raise his left hand and with his right hand placed on a Bible read out the Oath of Attestation;

" I Jesse Frederick Warren swear by Almighty God, that I will be faithful and bear true Allegiance to His Majesty King George the Fifth, His Heirs and Successors, and that I will, as in duty bound, honour and faithfully defend His Majesty, His Heirs and Successors. In Person, in

Crown and dignity against all enemies, and I will obey all orders of His Majesty, His Heirs and Successors and of the Generals and Officers set over me. So help me God."

The Sergeant dipped his pen into an inkwell and handed it to Jesse.

"Sign here" he said, pointing to a line at the bottom of the almost completed form of Attestation. An older bloke in a smart suit was sitting with the solider; both were to witness his signature.

Jesse took the pen, hesitating for a moment.

'This is it' he'd thought. Once he had put pen to paper and signed his name there would be no going back. A picture of Mill, soaking someone's unwanted crusts in watered down milk or gravy to keep her and their babies from starving had brought tears to his eyes and a lump had risen in his throat. Slowly he'd carefully added his signature and finalised the legal and binding document. It was not for King and Country he'd signed for but for young Millie, Cissy and his wife Mill. He never denied that because that was the truth. He was signing for them and for whatever lies ahead. Lord knows what would have become of them all if he hadn't.

'Well Mill,' he'd thought to himself as he handed the pen back, 'it's signed and sealed now girl, it's done. There'll be no stopping me now.'

The sergeant's voice seemed a long way off as he'd said,

"Sign here for your money and here are your certificates back" Jesse took the documents.

"This is the chit so your wife can claim her allowance from your pay and this is your rail pass for Sunday"

Jesse's mouth had dropped open, "Sunday?" he'd asked in disbelief, "where the bloody hell am I going Sunday?"

"You've been assigned to the Queen's Royal West Surrey's to start your basic training, their barracks are in Guildford. Report there by 16.00 hours this weekend and then you'll most likely be transferred to Hampshire".

Jesse felt he had been conned, "I haven't even told my Missus I've joined up yet!" he'd protested.

"Sorry chum but that's how it goes. From now on you're in the Army".

There was nothing Jesse could do about it.

"Sod that", he'd said to himself, feeling his anger rise as he walked from the behind the screens and headed towards the exit. He hadn't thought it would be that quick. Some blokes he'd known had waited three weeks before being called up. The thought of doing a runner did enter his mind, but like the sergeant had said, 'You're in the Army now' so there wasn't any chance of that.

The queue of would be volunteers had filled the entrance hall and was overflowing into the street. Jesse went into the urinals before leaving and as he came out held the door for a middle-aged gent who was going in. He wore a uniform from the Boar War,

"Not coming back for more are you dad?" Jesse had asked, his anger subsiding,

"Certainly am son," the man answered, "Did my bit for the old Queen, God bless her and I'll do it again for The King"

"Well, good luck to yer mate," Jesse said thinking the old chap must be barmy. Fancy wanting to go back for more!

He'd then pushed his way through the crowd and left the building.

By the time he reached Globe Road, he was frozen through, his foot was sore from the chaffing of the wet sock and he felt worn out. He had however, stopped at a grocer's in

Cambridge Heath Road and bought some eats, at least they would have a decent meal that night.

Jesse wearily climbed the steps up to 122, his wet boots squelching on the stone steps. This was going to be the hardest part of the day, He had to face Mill and tell her that he had joined up.

"You should have told me!" she cried after the initial shock, "What did you go and do that for, you might have got some work somewhere. There are plenty of unmarried men joining up every day. What do they want you for as well?"

Mill was now crying, young Milly started crying and so did the baby. "Look, Jesse said, "Let's get all these damp things off and we'll have some grub. Then we're talk about it later, see what's in the bag while I get some dry clobber on."

Holding baby Cissy on her hip, she pacified young Milly, "Come on Milly, let's see what Daddy has got in the bag, shall we?"

It was no good getting upset in front of the children, Jesse was right, they could talk about it later when the girls were asleep.

Young Milly eagerly climbed up onto a chair to see what was in the bag her father had left on the table. Mill had to admit it had been a long time since they had some decent food in the house; she tried not to let her daughters see the tears running down her face as she saw what Jesse had bought.

"Look Milly!" she exclaimed, "Your favourite rusks!" Young Milly didn't know they were her favourites, she had long forgotten what a rusk was. Mill opened the packet and gave her one.

She carried the baby to the bed and propped her up with large soft pillows to prevent her from falling. She was quite content to sit watching her mother and sister taking the goodies from the brown paper bag.

"Oh look!" exclaimed Mill as she lifted a crusty loaf from the bag, "we can have toast for our tea…oh and there's butter and look… a pot of jam!"

It had certainly been some time since they'd had the luxury of fresh bread, let alone butter as well. Young Milly, still biting on the rusk had found a bar of chocolate and handed it to her mother,

"Mummy, mummy, look, look!" she cried excitedly, not knowing what was inside the gaily coloured wrapper.

"Well that really is a special treat, it's chocolate" Mill told her daughter as she broke a piece off and gave it to her,

"Let's see what Cissy thinks of it, shall we?".

Milly followed her mother and jumped up onto the bed.

"Here you are sweetie", Mill said putting a tiny piece of chocolate into the baby's mouth, "we haven't forgotten you darling"

They sat on the bed, watching the baby "Now what do you think of that then?" their mother asked waiting for a reaction.

Cissy pulled a face at first but when she realised this new taste was nice, began crying for more. Mill smiled and young Milly giggled.

"All right, but just a little piece then, we don't want you being sick, do we?"

It was wonderful to be able to give the girls some little treat after the scraps they'd existed on. Mill was still feeding Cissy herself but she shuddered at the thought of what she, Jesse and Milly had been eating. She tried not to think about the toffs who hadn't finished their meal in the restaurant but then if they hadn't left something and if it hadn't been for young Billy....

Cissy began crying again and Mill put a dummy in her mouth, obviously the child had a liking for chocolate!

She cut two slices of bread and spread the butter, not bothering with the jam, she was that hungry. "Here Jesse!" she called, "come and eat this, I've cut you a slice".

While eating the bread she looked to see what else was in the bag. A small dark blue package contained 2oz of tea and in another there was sugar.

Mill like most women saved her morning tea grouts in a piece of muslin and tied it with a length of string. This she would infuse in boiling water throughout the day, although the last bag she had made had only just coloured the water making it look, as she would say, 'Like knat's water'. 'Well at least we can have a real decent strong cup for a change,' she said to herself and filled the kettle with fresh water from the enamel bucket they kept under the table. This saved having to keep going to tap on the landing which they shared with their neighbours.

Mill gave the fire a poke, added a knob of coal from the scuttle and placed the kettle on the trivet over the flames. She then went back to the table to cut another slice of bread. This time she added jam.

"Mmmm……" she said to Jesse who was tucking into the slice she had cut for him, "this is absolutely wonderful". He had to agree, apart from the Arrowroot biscuit, he'd not eaten since the day before and he suspected Mill hadn't had much more either.

Jesse had changed out of his damp clothes and hung them over the backs of the fireside chairs to dry. He was glad to feel the warmth of the room and the comfort of a dry pair of socks. It had been a very eventful day and they had a lot to talk about but for now he just wanted to enjoy the moment. What more could a man want than to see his family eating food that was fresh and not having to suffer the shame and humiliation of depending on left offs only fit for feeding pigs, to hear his eldest daughter giggling happily as she played with a simple little doll and see his baby sleeping contentedly.

He watched as Mill made a pot of tea, she seemed to have got over her initial surprise of the unexpected announcement he'd blurted out or maybe she was like him, waiting for the right the moment to talk about it? However he dreaded having to tell her he would be leaving at the weekend. He'd tell her all about the day's outcome later, but he'd leave the worst to last. If there was going to be a scene, then he'd rather it not be here.

"How about going for a drink in the Greyhound tonight?" he suggested, "There's a few coppers left from my joining up money and we haven't been out for ages".

"Well, it would be nice to go out for once" Mill answered, "but how much have you got left? Can we afford it?" she asked, "We don't want to waste it"

"If we just have one, we'll be O.K." he told her, "We've got to sort some things out and we can't talk here without waking the girls".

"Alright then" she agreed and said she would see if their neighbour Hetty Samuels would keep an eye on the children.

"Has she heard anything from John lately?"

"Yes, she had a card this morning, just said he was alright and would write again when he settled"

"Did she say where he is?"

"No, but I think he is still doing his training"

Jesse felt a bit uneasy; he still couldn't believe he would be going off himself within a few days. Perhaps he and John might meet up somewhere; it would certainly be great to bump into his old mate again but he thought it very unlikely.

He cut himself another slice of bread and Mill poured the tea and after a second cup she made the effort to get up from where she had been sitting on the bed. "I'll just pop up and see Hetty then", Milly lifted her arms up to her mother, "Oh, come on then, I'll take you with me"

She looked at the baby who was sleeping peacefully and as she was about to leave the room turned towards Jesse saying,

"I don't like it Jesse, you joining up, I only wish there was some other way" she left before he saw the tears of sorrow slowly running down her cheeks.

'So do I' he thought 'so do I'.

"Hetty's gone to her mother's", Jesse had fallen asleep in one of the fireside chairs and awoke as he heard Mill come back into the room. "But Mrs Johnson said she'd look after the girls. She ain't expecting any babies to be born tonight and she said that if any-one pegs it, then they'll have to wait 'til morning to be laid out." Jesse laughed, "Well, don't suppose it'll make much difference to them when they're seen to. Won't know much about it any way, will they? When yer dead, yer dead."

"Oh, and I told her you've joined up" Mill added as an afterthought looking at him disapprovingly.

'Christ!' Jesse thought, 'let's get down the pub'.

The Greyhound was rather quiet that evening, but then it was only Tuesday. The busiest nights were Saturdays when those who were still lucky enough to be working would more often than not, be spending a bit of their earnings and leisure time with their drinking mates. Many spent more money in the pubs than they could really afford and then had the wife to contend with when they did eventually roll home.

It was nothing unusual to hear babies crying late into the night as arguing neighbours kept them awake after chucking out time. Especially as there was also the Camel Public House further along Globe Road and every now and again a window in the buildings or terraced houses opposite would open as an irate neighbour shouted,

"For Christ sake pack yer bloody row up! We're trying to get some kip in 'ere!"

Then another window opened and a voice would shout back,

"Sod off and mind yer own business!"

This tempted a challenge,

"Do yer wan'na say that down in the street?" would come a
reply, quickly followed by a woman's shrill voice screaming,
"Git in ere you daft ol' sod and shut that flipping window!
Do yer wan' us to freeze to bloody death!"
Then if it they were lucky, the street would settle down and
go back to sleep.

Mill and Jesse entered the pub by the side entrance having
walked past the main door that led into the Saloon Bar and
the door for the Public Bar. The Saloon was for the 'snobs'
or those that liked more comfortable surroundings. The
Public Bar was where most people gathered on a Saturday
night because that's where the piano was and they all
enjoyed having a singsong together. It was also in the Public
where the fights usually started, which of course was all part
of the evening's entertainment and it wasn't always the men.
Sometimes the women got into an argument and then they
would have a right ol' set to. Tonight was no exception for as

Mill and Jesse headed for the smaller room at the far end of the building known as the Snug a shrill voice was heard screaming, "Leave my ol' man alone you ol' trollop! I've seen yer givin' 'im the eye."

"Shut up you daft cow, what would I want your bloody ol' man for? Got enough of me own so what the hell would I want yours for an all? Any way from wot yeah said the other day he ain't no good for you so he won't be any good to me!| At least I like a man who knows what he's got it for. Your ol'd man ain't got it in him anymore! He can just about manage to raise his ale let alone any fing else"

A man voice, no doubt belonging to the first woman's husband retaliated with, "'Ere Maude, wot yer been saying about me?"

"Oh shut up and get on with 'yer pint, I'm off 'ome!"

It didn't matter what door you went in by, you still couldn't miss the smell; stale beer, cheap perfume, tobacco smoke and a whiff from the urinals all mixed together. You could always smell the latter, even though they were out the back. The smell reminded Jesse of the Recruiting Office he'd been to earlier in the day.

They made their way into the Snug and Jesse went up to the bar for the drinks; a port and lemon for Mill and ha'pint of Ben Truman's for himself.

"Thanks mate", Jesse said to the barman as he lifted the beer and took a sip, 'Blimey', he said to himself as he licked his lips, 'That's bloody marvellous!' It had been some weeks since he had been in the Greyhound and the beer tasted great.

"Ain't seen yer in 'ere lately" said the Landlord inquiring after Jesse, "thought you'd gone and joined up"

"Yer, I have mate" he replied, "went and did it today. Didn't have much choice really, we need the money."

The Landlord wished him all the best and told him there'd be a pint waiting for him when he got back. "Thanks chum, let's hope it will all be over soon and I'll keep you to that promise!"

"Well don't tell the others" the Landlord joked, "they'll all be signing on if they think there's a free pint in it!"

Jesse made his way over to where Mill was sitting at one of the half dozen or so small round wooden tables and gave her the port and lemon He hoped they didn't end up having a 'barney' before the night was out. There was no point in arguing now, he'd signed his name and made his allegiance to the King. Whatever Mill said wouldn't change that.

Although The Greyhound was partitioned into the three sections by wood panelling and etched glass windows one long bar served the three rooms and even that had glass partitions across the polished counter. Being the Snug was the smallest of the three rooms and at the far end, it only had a short bar. The drinks were cheaper in there and the room was cosier. Mill always preferred it in there, but when Jesse was with his mates, he used the Public. The Snug was usually where the women liked to sit and natter, while the men were enjoying themselves next door, or for those folk who wanted a quiet drink before any ructions started.

A small wood burning stove against the wall opposite the bar was alight and throwing out some warmth. The large brass ornate gas lamp hanging overhead hissed as it sent out a yellowish glow.

Red flocked wallpaper with a paisley design in gold covered the upper half of the walls and the dark wood panelling continued around the bottom half. Heavy gold tasselled curtains were drawn across the only window and there were several pictures of cattle standing in rivers adorning the walls. The floor although now badly marked and scuffed had once been stained dark oak, as were the tables and wheel back chairs.

Mill kept her hat on and having removed her coat was sitting near the stove.

Two elderly couples sitting together in the corner were the only other people in there. They nodded to Jesse as he removed his cap and coat.

He sat down, with his back to the middle of the room

"All the best love," he said raising his glass to Mill, "let's hope this flipping war gets sorted out soon and we can all get back to normal"

Before Mill could answer a slurred voice said, "And …I'll drink to that. Hic….and to the King, God Bless…hic….. 'em all"

An elderly woman, swaying drunkenly on her feet had come into the Snug and was standing behind Jesse. Bright orange frizzy dyed hair stuck out from under an old black bowler hat with a moth eaten bunch of cherries hanging from the brim. She had a tatty brown shawl around her shoulders and bright red spots of rouge on her checks.

"Yeah, all the best luv", Jesse said humouring the woman as she almost fell over a chair, "mind yer don't fall over ma"

"It won't….be…hic….the first time…I've fell arse over 'ed mate", she answered trying to steady herself by holding onto a table, "I only came in 'ere looking for me ol' man….don't know where the old sod's got to…hic.." and with that she stumbled off unsteadily and went out into the street..

"Perhaps he's joined up," Mill said quietly looking into her drink.

Jesse knew she was digging at him but he didn't answer until he'd taken another swig of beer. He took a deep breath; there was no point in stalling,

"You know I had to do it Mill, don't yer? There's just nothing going. What else was there? You know I've tried hard enough to get work. How do you think I feel, watching you trying to keep us all going on someone's scrapes of food? It breaks my heart Mill, honest it does". He put his glass down on the table and absentmindedly placed it in one of the many rings that had stained the table over the years. I could make a good job of re-polishing that he thought to himself.

"I know Jesse" Mill was saying, "it's not your fault there's a war on," she cried, "but joining the Army! Why didn't you tell me where you were going?"

"You know very well why I didn't, you would have done your pieces and we would have 'ad a flaming great row. You don't think I want to go do yer? This way we'll have a few bob coming in each week", he explained, "and then you and the girls can have some decent grub for a change, Lord knows you deserve it. I'm not 'aving my family living off other people's plates Mill. That's not what I want for you," he stopped for a moment remembering how it was when he was a kid, "I'm not having you and the little ones living the way I did. It's all signed and sealed, they've accepted me and I'm in the Army now or at least soon will be"

What do you mean, soon will be? When are you going then?"

"Sunday", he replied quietly

"Sunday!" Mill shouted jumping up from her seat and knocking the table with her leg.

"'Ere, mind me beer!" Jesse said lifting his glass.

"Sod the bloody beer!" she retaliated, "How come you're off so quick? You'll be gone before I even get used to the idea!"

The elderly people sitting in the corner were looking over with interest.

"That's it dearie, you tell 'im", one of the men called.

"Yeah, he wants to stay where 'e is if it's anything like the last lot we were in", said the other, both obviously old soldiers from the Boar Wars.

"Oh, sit down Mill" Jesse told her giving the old boys a menacing look.

Mill did as she was bid hoping Jesse would ignore the comments from the two men. This was just how arguments started and she didn't want any trouble tonight.

Jesse slowly supped his beer; he'd only got half a pint and wanted it to last a while yet.

"Look" he said, wiping the back of his hand across his mouth, "I ain't too keen about this me self, but I ain't the only one. You should have seen em down the Recruiting Office today", he took another sip, "some of 'em are just kids"

"Yes, but they're not married are they?"

"No, I don't suppose they were, but loads of the other blokes were".

He went on to tell Mill about this chap named Bert who he'd met and made Mill smile at the thought of all the wet drawers hanging all over the pace.

"I've seen enough of that myself back home, what with all my lot," she told him referring to her mother's house in Walthamstow, "still, I suppose they've got to dry them somewhere in this weather"

Jesse wasn't really interested in where females hung their wet drawers so he went on to tell her about the woman who came in looking for her son. He also told Mill about the medical he'd had and the name of the regiment he was now assigned to,

"I'm in the Queen's Royal West Surrey's", he told her.

It was the first time he had ever actually said the name and thought it sounded rather impressive.

"Well who are they when they're at home then?" Mill asked.

"It's a Surrey Regiment, don't know much about them me self really" he answered almost adding 'no doubt I soon will', but thought better of it.

"They've got a lamb carrying a flag as their Regiments badge……" he began but suddenly had a thought, "That's it!" he exclaimed, "That's it!"

"What are you on about?" Mill asked looking bewildered.

"The lamb! That's it! When I was going in, two blokes were coming out and one said, 'See yer in the Mutton Lancers', I thought it was the name of a pub but I guess it's a nickname of sort. Get it?" he asked Mill. "Lamb? Mutton?"

"I'm not daft Jesse. More like a lamb being led to the slaughter if yer ask me".

"Oh, come on Mill, it's not going to be like that. I've heard blokes say there's going to be a big push soon and it'll all be over before we know it."

"Oh yeah, and that'll be the day when bread's a penny a' hundredweight and coals a ha'penny a loaf!" She always said this when doubtful about anything, "and" she went on, "what about all those Regulars who have gone down already, poor souls." She had a taste of her port and lemon before adding, "Now they want to send the ordinary blokes out there too, something must be up"

"I know, that was terrible", he replied, "but as I heard it there ain't a lot of the Jerries left now, they say our boys took a lot with 'em. This big push we hear about is just to flush 'em all out and finish it all off. You see", he said trying to convince her and himself, "it will all be back to normal soon, it can't last much longer".

"Well I hope your right Jesse, I really do".

They sat talking, making their drinks last as long as they could. Jesse explained about the joining up procedure and about the allowance she would get each week.

There was enough money to keep them going for a day or two, but that would be it. Hopefully Mill could rely on Mrs. Johnson's son to see them through until she cashed her first allowance voucher the following week.

Jesse was relieved that she had now accepted the idea of him joining up even though she didn't want him to go, but she knew he had been right. They would never have survived this long if it hadn't been for Billy. If he went and volunteered as well, then there would be nothing for them to eat. When things were back to normal he'd make it up to that generous and thoughtful lad.

They stayed for a while to finish their drinks and were just about to get up to leave when they heard a familiar voice,

"Oh, 'ere yer are then," a woman was saying, "they said you were down the pub"

"Well, blow me!" Jesse said surprised, "Aunt Amy, what you doing down this way!"

Jesse had kept in touch with his aunt since he and Mill married four years back, but it had been a while since he'd last seen her.

"Here, sit down", he said pulling another chair to the table, "What are you doing in this neck of the woods?"

His aunt went on to tell them how one of her neighbours had been chucked out for not paying the rent and was now living with a cousin just round the corner from Jesse.

"Someone I know has got the use of a horse and cart so I've got him to bring me mates stuff over," she said, "but it had to be done tonight, 'cause he's joined up and has to be away by to-morrow". She didn't miss the look Mill and Jesse gave each other,

"Any how" she went on "I thought I'd come over with 'em and pop in to see how yer doing, I've got about half an hour while they unload"

Jesse felt uncomfortable not being able to buy his aunt a drink

"It's all right son", she said as Jesse made apologies, "here go and get another round, I'm feeling a bit flushed today". She opened a large tapestry bag, fished out her purse and gave him some coins, "These are on me and I'll have a gin and orange son"

Jesse went off to the bar.

After taking her gloves off and the fox fur she wore around her neck Amy loosened her coat then turned her attention to Mill, "Lovely baby you've got back there Mill", she said thumbing back towards Gratton Houses, "and young Milly's grown since I saw her last"

"Did you go in then?"

"Just for a minute, your neighbour told me Jesse's signed up then?"

Mill sniffed as she felt tears filling her eyes. "He went and did it this afternoon, never even told me he was going,"

"You know Mill", Amy tried to comfort her and patted her arm, "he seems real tough sometimes, but he's got a heart of gold underneath. He thinks the world of you and the girls so don't be too hard on him".

Mill blew her nose as Jesse returned with the drinks,

"So you've joined up then?"

She listened as Jesse told her about the events of the day and then asked Mill what she was going to do when he had gone,

"Will you stay on here?"

Neither of them had thought about that and Mill and Jesse looked at each other.

"I don't know, I suppose I will", Mill answered. "What do you think Jesse?"

"We do owe some back rent, it might be an idea if we could find somewhere else," he suggested.

Amy had an idea "I'll tell you what, why don't you go back to Walthamstow, there's a lot of places empty over there you know and the rent's pretty cheap? Your sister Annie's been living there since she married that Arthur Fulshaw fellow, she told me it's somewhere near the Higham Hill Tavern.

Jesse enquired after his sister who like his aunt, he had only seen occasionally over the last few years.

"She moved to Walthamstow when Granny Clarke and her family decided to go there, some months back"

"Haven't seen Granny Clark for ages now" Jesse said, recalling it was her who looked after Annie when their mother had died.

"She's doing alright" Amy went on, "you know her daughter Emily?" Jesse nodded having slight recollections of her, "Well she's married a chap named Albert Simmons, he's in the Regular Army, joined up about three years back. She's got a baby now, a boy. I think they named him Albert as well." She went on to tell them that they too were now living in Walthamstow, "They were living in Brummer Road, but......"

Before she could finish telling them what she had to say, Mill hearing the name of a familiar street cried,

"Oh, I know where that is, it's just around the corner from where my lot live in Cranbrook Road. They're on one side of Southgrove Road and Brummer is on the other. Just down a bit on the left" she added.

Jesse nodded; he knew where Mill meant because he remembered the Artful, a decent pub at the bottom of Brummer Road.   Nearby was where the junction of Southgrove, Markhouse Road and St James's Street met. On the corner of Markhouse Road was the Brewery Tap Tavern and opposite that stood the Essex Brewery where they brewed the ale. In his mind Jesse savoured the aroma of the fermenting hops.

He could almost see the clouds of sweet smelling steam bellowing from the tall chimneys way above the brewery. He remembered another Public House named the Coach and Horses was just around the bend in St. James's Street. Yes, Jesse knew where Mill meant all right, he'd tried out most of the pubs in the area with her father Joseph, just before he and Mill had wed.

 "Yeah," he said with a sigh, almost licking his lips at the thought, "I know where yer mean".

"Well," his aunt was saying as she continued the story, "with Albert away in the Army, Emilys now gone down somewhere called Glenthorne Road and is living next door but one to her mother".

"That's just off Blackhorse Road" Mill told them airing her knowledge of the district. Jesse looked a bit puzzled,

"You know Jesse" Mill prompted, "it's just past the bottom of the High Street, about two turnings passed Coppermill Lane, over on the left"

Jesse had an idea where this road was because he knew the High Street with its mile long market and another two pubs came to mind, The Chequers and The Cock Tavern. He took a sip of his beer, "Why don't you go over to your mother's" he suggested "and see how the land lies? It might be a good idea."

Mill hadn't been on very good terms with her mother since she'd married Jesse. Her mother had always been dead set against any of her children marrying, whether it be the boys or girls but more so with Mill. Being the eldest she had always been expected to be helping with the enormous piles of washing, ironing and cooking that went with sixteen children.

It was taken for granted that Mill looked after the whole family while her mother continually produced more offspring. It had been many months before Mill and her mother were on speaking terms again.

"I'll think about it," Mill said as they all got up to leave.

Outside was very dark, the air hung thick with smoke and fog as usual, but at least the snow had lain off. They all shivered as they came out from the warmth of the pub and the cold air hit them. A horse and cart stood waiting in the road, two dim lanterns were attached either side of the wide seat. Mill said her goodbyes to Aunt Amy and went on ahead so that Mrs. Johnson could get off home.

Jesse helped his aunt up onto the seat, the chap who had come to collect her was well wrapped up against the weather and handed Amy a couple of blankets.

"Will you be alright" Jesse asked, "its freezing tonight and dark"

"She'll be O.K. mate", the driver told him, "Ol' Daisy 'ere knows her way 'ome blindfolded, won't take us long".

"This weather ain't killed me off yet, Amy was saying, "reckon I'm used to it by now, Oh, this is Alfred by the way" she said as she wrapped herself in the blankets, "I told you about him, he's joined up too"

"Well all the best to yer mate," Jesse said, "might see you around some time"

The driver released the brake; "Giddy-up" he called to the horse and flicked the reins. Daisy started to move off, "Bye now son, look after yourself," his aunt called… "an' we'll meet up again when it's all over" then they were on their way. Jesse watched as they set off along Globe Road and then made his way back to Gratton Houses. The wet was seeping into his boot again and he felt weary. He stood for a moment before entering the building and watched as the cart disappeared into the gloomy night. That morning he'd been standing there watching the coal man with his horses and cart coming along the road towards him and now at the end of the day, he was watching another cart leaving. As he turned to go back into the dwellings he thought how quickly his life had changed since he had left that morning. Then he had been just an ordinary East End bloke; tonight he was Private Jesse Warren, a member of His Majesty's Armed Forces. He had no idea what lie ahead of him or how it would all end but he knew whatever the outcome, February 15th 1915 would certainly be a day to remember.

Chapter Four

The following Sunday Jesse said his goodbyes to his two daughters before Mill took them along to Hetty's. She would mind them while Mill went to see him off at Bethnal Green Station, just around the corner in Cambridge Heath Road.

While Jesse waited for Mill to come back he looked around the room that had been their home for the last three years. He remembered young Milly being born there and then the following year Cissy had come along both being delivered in the bedroom they could no longer afford to use. He smiled as he thought of how Mrs. Johnson had sent him off to the Greyhound when Milly was being born and then sent her Billy running in shouting, "It's a girl!, It's a girl!" Everyone had patted him on the back and plied him with drink. And then later when Cissy had arrived, the lad had run in again shouting excitedly. "It's another girl! You've got another daughter.

He had hoped one day for a son to make his family complete, but who knows what would happen now. Even though he'd almost convinced himself he may not even go to France, he knew deep in his heart that it was highly likely. So many men had already been killed; many of them trained professional soldiers as well as the earlier volunteers. Jesse wondered how he would cope if he had to go to the battlefields of France or even Belgium. Would he be one of the lucky one's he wondered. Would he come back and one day hear some-one calling to him, "It's a boy! You've got a son!" He prayed it would be so. Not only did he pray for himself, but also for all the thousands of men already out there and for those about to leave their homes and loved ones like he was doing today.

Admittedly he had joined up for the money, but if he could do his bit in getting this dumbfounded war over and done with, then he would. He hoped all this talk of a war to end all wars turns out the way the 'Big-wigs' and politicians prophesied 'and if we are all sent out there'... well, he didn't want to think about that any more.

The door opened, "Alright then Jesse?" Mill asked indicating that it was time to leave.

He picked up the small attaché case she had packed for him. Neither of them had much idea as to what he would need to take. However, Mill had put in his two sets of clean underwear, all the socks he possessed, several handkerchiefs and his shaving gear. Without her knowing, he'd added the photo she'd had taken just after they married.

He looked around the room for the last time,

"Yes girl, let's get going."

She held on tightly to Jesse's arm as they walked to the station. It was snowing and the wind whipped Mill's long scarf against her face. She snuggled up to Jesse but neither of them spoke, there was no need for words.

The painful time of parting grew closer with every step they took. Both were trying desperately not to let the other see the tears in their eyes. As Jesse pulled Mill closer to him his heart was aching. He wanted to scream, 'It's not right! It's not fair! How can I leave her like this?" but he knew there was no answer, he had to go.

'What if I am sent to France?' he asked himself, 'Supposing I don't get back, supposing I never see her and the girls again?' He tried to push these uncomfortable thoughts to the back of his mind, but he felt an icy fear creeping over him.

He knew Mill would be all right now that she had decided to leave Gratton Houses but how would she know what was happening? He didn't even have an address yet for her to write to. Hopefully her mother would put her up until she found a place to stay. After all, hadn't Aunt Amy told them there were a lot of places to rent in that area?

Jesse was glad Amy had come along that evening because Mill had taken her advice and had decided to go back to Walthamstow. This gave him some reassurance; at least she would have her family nearby.

Mill told Jesse she should wait until she got her first weeks allowance and then take the girls in the pram by train. He suggested she should leave young Milly and Cissy with her mother or one of her sisters and find a carrier who would bring her back to collect their belongings or at least what they had left of them.

"Perhaps one of your brother's will come with you?" he'd suggested.

She agreed to this and Jesse was relieved, he knew she would be all right at her mothers for a while, especially as she'd have a bit of money to pay her way.

"Get away as soon as you can Mill", he told her, "otherwise the rent collector will be banging on the door for his money. We only owe a couple of weeks so he can go whistle for it. They've got more money than we have and after all…." he paused and as if he could forget, "there is a war on".

He was trying to make Mill feel better about the fact that she would have to do what was commonly known as a 'Moonlight Flit' an expression used for families who tried to flee before the rent collector called. "If he bangs on the door before you leave, just don't answer it".

By now they had reached the end of Old Ford Road and had turned into Cambridge Heath Road.

"Look at this lot!" Mill said, surprised at the crowds of people heading towards the station. Normally Sunday morning was very quiet, but like Jesse, those who had volunteered throughout the week were off to join various Regiments. And like Mill, their families and loved one's were there to see them off.

Jesse showed his pass at the station entrance and the ticket inspector waved Mill through as well. No one was bothering with platform tickets today.

They climbed the steps leading up to the platform, Jesse's train was due in at 10.30 a.m. Mill looked at the huge clock hanging above the platform; they had just ten minutes to say their goodbyes.

All around women with young children and babies stood quietly with their men folk, young sweethearts were embracing oblivious of no-one but each other. Middle aged couples were talking softly to younger lads, probably their sons. Elderly folk were there too, Mill had never seen so many people on the station. Some men were already in uniform, no doubt heading back to their regiments after a short pass.

A large group of lads further down near the end of the platform were standing about with their families. Jesse told Mill they looked like the youngsters he had seen at the Recruiting Office.

"They join up together to be in the same Regiment, they call 'em the 'Pals' Brigade' because a lot of 'em come from the same colleges and many worked in the same department stores or offices and the factories".

Mill never answered for someone had called; "It's coming!" and a murmur went around the platform.

The whole place shook when the massive noisy steam engine pulled into the station, screeching and squealing like a great fiery monster as the driver applied the brakes. Black smoke bellowing from the funnel sent smuts and soot upward into the falling snow. The crowds stood back as the train came to a final halt. Those standing near the front of the train were suddenly lost from view as clouds of white vapour and steam, hissing from deep within the very bowels of the engine engulfed them. Children started screaming and clung to their mother's skirts, petrified that this enormous terrifying giant was coming to get them.

Doors were being thrown open; already other volunteers from the previous stations were on board and looking out from the grimy carriage windows.

Jesse put his arms around Mill and held her tight; there was no stopping her tears now.

"Look after you'self Mill, give the girls a kiss for me every night, won't you?" He felt a hard lump in his throat and thought he would choke, he swallowed hard. He felt her wet tears on his face as she whispered,

"Come back to us Jesse, God keep you safe".

"I'll be alright Mill, you know me, tough as old boots", he said trying to make her smile. "Look I'm only going for the training; I might be able to get home now and again. I won't be that far away".

He held her away from him and looked into her tearful face,

"Do you know what I reckon?" She shook her head,

"One day when we're old, we'll sit and tell our grandchildren all about today and this rotten war. One day we'll look back on all this, just you wait and see Mill," he went on, trying to hold back his own tears, "just you wait and see"

"Well, we will certainly have something to tell 'em; thank goodness the girls are too young to understand what's going on".

"Yeah, but we'll tell 'em about it one day, when they're older"

"Jesse, I'm so proud of what you're doing, I know if it weren't for me and the girls.......'

Doors were being banged shut,

"All aboard!" called the guard, "Mind the doors....all aboard!"

Jesse pulled Mill close once more wishing he could hold her forever., "I love you Mill" he said no longer keeping back the tears, "I love you Mill, look after the girls, tell them I love them". He kissed her one last time and let go of her to board the train. She clung to his hand as he leant from the open window,

"I love you!" she cried, "Write to me, won't you? I'll be at my mother's!

As the fireman stoked up the coal the engine driver let two ear-shattering blasts from the train's whistle. She couldn't hear what Jesse was saying.

The guard, leaning from the van at the rear end of the train blew his whistle as he waved a green flag. The huge wheels began to turn slowly and then the gigantic engine jerked violently and started to move, taking with it the men and lads of London's East End. These were the brave and gallant volunteers of London. They were leaving their homes, some their jobs and especially their loved ones to face an unknown future. For most it would be their first experience of being away from the only life they had ever known. For many it would be their last.

As the train pulled out of the station, all the windows of the carriages were lowered as men tried to get a final glimpse of their families. Many of them would never come back and this would be their last goodbye forever.

Jesse had let Mill's fingers slip from his hand. She waved until the train disappeared into the murky London weather. "Please God", she prayed, "bring him home safely, bring them all home safely."

Jesse sat back and closed his eyes, he knew there were tears running down his face, but he didn't care. Other men were feeling the same; many were blowing their noses trying not to show their emotions. He wanted to keep their last precious moments together in his mind. He had no idea when or even if, he would ever see his wife again and as the train gathered speed it took him further and further away.

Like many other women left standing on the platform, Mill wept all the way home. In just five days her whole world had been turned upside down.

When she got back to Gratton Houses she went straight to no 126, her friend Hettys.

"Come on in Mill" Hetty said when she opened the door, "Get your coat off while I pour you a nice cuppa. "The girls are all right; my eldest is playing with them.

Mill did as she was bid and sat down wiping her nose and still sniffing.

"Now come on Mill, he'll be all right, just you wait and see" Hetty handed her a cup of tea, "I know how you're feeling luv, I worry sick about my John."

"I know" Mill replied, grateful for the hot tea. "Why do we have to have a war?" she blurted out to her friend, "We were all doing alright before...why do they want our men" she cried, "What do they know about it all?"

"I don't know luv", Hetty replied, "I wish I did" she sighed, "these things happen. Maybe it will all be over soon. My John said it wouldn't last much longer. Now come on drink your tea," she said kindly.

They both sat quietly for a few minutes, both with their own thoughts.

Mill was the first to speak,

"I'm moving out Hetty, I'm going back to Walthamstow.

"Oh, Mill, I am sorry to 'ear that, is it 'cos of the rent?"

"Yes, we owe two weeks and I won't have any money until next week when I can get the Army Allowance"

"Can't you hang on 'til then Mill?" her friend asked sympathetically, "The ol' rent knocker won't be calling again 'til Friday afternoon, perhaps he'll wait for a while?"

"Even if he does, I won't be able to pay the back rent, no I've made up my mind and besides I've promised Jesse I'd go."

Hetty put more boiling water into the teapot, "When were you thinking of going Mill?" she asked.

"This afternoon,".

"This afternoon!" Hetty cried, "yer can't go just like that! What about all yer stuff?"

"I've thought about it and I want to get away as soon as I can".

"What about the train fare, 'ave yer got *any* money?"

"No" said Mill, "I'm going to walk."

"Walk!" Hetty was aghast, "Mill it's nearly seven miles to Walthamstow! Yer can't walk in this weather…an' what about the girls, it's been snowing!?"

"They'll be alright in the pram, I'll wrap 'em up well and put a hot water bottle in their blankets".

"Does Jesse know you're doing this?"

"No, he thinks I am going to wait for the money before I go".

"Oh, Mill, I wish I could help yer out luv. I've only got tu'pence to last all week me self".

"It's alright Hetty, don't worry. I'll be O.K. I'll take whatever I can today and try to borrow a couple of shillings when I get home. There's a carter who's got the stables round near my mother's, someone will bring me back with a cart for our stuff."

"But where will yer store it all? Yer got to put it somewhere girl"

Mill had already thought about that, "Old Mr Bailey, the bloke who owns the stables, he'll probably have some space, used to 'ave several horses at one time but last time I was there someone said he only 'ad two now.

"What's yer mum going to say when yer turn up? Are fings better with you an 'er now?"

"Well, I've seen her on and off a couple of times but she's still not really forgiven me for getting married an' leaving her but it's just 'ard luck, the other girls are there so she's got plenty of help, besides, I ain't got anywhere else to go"

Hetty went over to her small kitchen range, "Here Mill" 'ave some of this broth, there ain't much in it, just some veg but there's plenty 'ere for you and young Milly. You'll need something in yer girl."

"Oh, Hetty" Mill started crying again, "You've been such a good friend to me, I'll come back and see you when this is all over"

"I 'ope yer do, but you an' Jesse 'ave been good mates to me an' my John too so don't forget that."

Hetty offered to look after the girls while Mill sorted out what she was taking with her.

First she went up to see Mrs. Johnson who like Hetty was shocked at Mill's intentions and tried to talk her out of going. It was no use though; she had made up her mind and wanted to leave as soon as she could.

"O.K. luvey, I just wish there was somefink I could do to 'elp out, I'm stony broke me'self".

"Oh, Mrs Johnson!" Mill cried throwing her arms around the older woman, "You brought me babies into the world and if it wasn't for your Billy, we would 'ave all starved to death."

"There, there, dearie, we all 'elp each other out when we can. Billy's gone off to work, he'll be sorry not to say goodbye".

"You know we'll never ever forget your kindness Mrs Johnson, you an' your lad kept us going. As long as I live, I swear I'll always remember yer."

"Go on, don't be daft girl. Come in an' see me when you come back for yer stuff, won't yer?" Mill promised she would and went back to see what she could find room for in the pram

Two hours later she was ready for the long walk she had in front of her. The big bassinet pram was loaded. It had a storage compartment under the mattress and Mill had filled it with as many nappies and baby clothes that would squeeze in. The linen from young Milly's cot and Cissy's basket was folded and laid flat over the prams mattress. One big pillow was behind the girls who were now in the pram side by side. A stone hot water bottle was wrapped in a towel to keep the girls warm and both were tucked up well against the weather. Mill pulled the hood of the pram up and attached a muslin cover over the front. This she hoped would protect the children from the smoke and fog and finally secured the rainproof storm cover.

Behind the pillow she had put two babies' bottles full of hot milk and the last half of a loaf she had brought the day before. If young Milly got hungry she could have a piece of that. At the foot of the pram were her personal documents and papers. Jesse had given her back the certificates he had taken and these would be going with her today for safe keeping. She had put extra clothes on the girls and she herself wore two skirts over an extra layer of flannel underwear.

After locking the door of number 122 she made sure the key was safely in her handbag. Mill tucked the bag behind the pillow at the back of the pram along with the babies' bottles.

She wore the only coat she possessed. It was dark brown with a small fur collar and matching cuffs. The coat almost reached her ankles. She'd put her long woollen scarf over her head, tied it under her chin and with the ends hanging down her back, tucked into the belt of the coat. The high button boots were not ideal footwear for walking seven miles or so, but that was all she had. At least she hoped they would keep the wet out and she wore her extra thick stockings.

She noticed it had stopped snowing and although everywhere looked very pretty and picturesque it wouldn't stay like that, it never did. Soon it would all turn black as soot and smoke drifted down from the heavy polluted atmosphere, crunching underfoot before turning into wet sludge.

Hetty and Mrs Johnson, wrapped in their knitted shawls came to the main entrance to say their goodbyes.

After pulling on woollen gloves, she carefully lowered the pram down the front step of Gratton House and then onto the pavement. It was going to be hard pushing the pram through this lot but her mind was made up and she was all set to go.

The two women watching her leave were both sorry to see her going like this. They had all been friends since Mill and Jesse had moved in and had shared some good times together and more recently some bad times but the war had changed everything now. They knew Mill was doing what she thought was best.

"Mind how yer go dearie" Mrs Johnson called out as Mill turned to give them a wave, "We'll see yer tomorrow then? Come in for a cuppa when yer come back for your stuff" Mill promised she would and with a few more 'Goodbye's made her way towards Old Ford Road and the start of her long trek. Although she did have every intention of returning the following day with a carrier for her belongings, things didn't quite go according to her plans. After her arduous journey pushing the pram through the wet slush and sometimes in places over frozen snow that had not yet thawed, she arrived at Cranbrook Road, her old family home absolutely exhausted and on the verge of collapse.

For over three hours she had kept going, despite her thick stockings her boots had rubbed the back of her heels and were very sore. The bitter cold had seeped through her layers of clothing, chilling her body to the bone. During the long stretch along Lea Bridge Road that had taken them from Bethnal Green and up towards Markhouse Road it had started snowing again making the journey even more laborious. Mill tried walking in the road but as the snow fell heavier it became difficult to see the oncoming trams and other horse drawn traffic that was about. At one point when the small wheels at the front of the pram had stuck in the snow building up against the kerb, a kindly old gentleman had helped and between them they had the pram back onto the pavement.

She just kept walking and pushing as the icy snow fell on her face. She tried brushing the snow from the pram; thankfully both girls were sleeping well tucked down under the covers but it was useless brushing the snow for it soon settled again. 'Just keep going…. just keep going' she said whispering to herself as she struggled on. By the time she turned into Markhouse Road it was late in the afternoon and already dark but thankfully it had stopped snowing.

Lights shone from the windows of the grand houses that occupied this end. It was here that the doctors, accountants, lawyers and other professional people lived. These properties were very impressive with huge stone lions resting on either side of the steps that led up to the front of the houses. It was as if they were guarding the occupants who lived there safely tucked behind the heavy doors. The girls were getting restless now and young Milly was trying to get up. She stopped for a while and gave her a rusk and one of the bottles of now slightly warm milk that she'd brought with her. After giving the baby some milk from the other bottle she tucked them both well in under the covers and started off again, she had to keep going.

She passed St. Saviours Church on her left and could see its magnificent steeple through the snow and the beautiful stained glass window alive with colour from the lights inside church. Mill wondered why the church was open today, but then remembered it was Sunday. No doubt many would soon be leaving the comfort of their firesides to go along to Evening Song. There were a lot of prayers to be said that night for all the loved ones who were away from home and now facing unknown dangers in the battlefields of France and Belgium.

Mill's arms felt like they had been pulled from their sockets. The muscles in her shoulders and back of the neck were really hurting from the strain of pushing; sometimes she found it easier to pull the pram behind her. Her clothes were soaked through and she was bitterly cold. Desperately, she wished she were at her mothers. Just keep going….. just keep going…. I've got to make it, she kept repeating to herself.

By the time she had reached the Lighthouse Methodist Church about half a mile further she felt relief, 'not much further, not much further'

She crossed here and passed the Common Gate Public House on her right and to where the lights from the long row of shops shone onto the pavement in front. Thankfully the shop keepers had been out clearing the snow which made it so much easier for people passing by and potential customers but little did Mill know, as she passed this row of shops, that one day in the future she would be living in one of these properties for over twenty years.

"Nearly there girls", she said to her sleeping daughters, "nearly at Grandma's' She was feeling breathless and very, very tired. 'Just keep going… just keep going…' she told herself.

When at last she turned right into Arkley Road she knew she was almost there, just through the alleyway on her left and then past the stables. A horse shiered as she passed, banging its hoofs against the stable doors making Mill jump as the doors were pushed out, straining against the bolts. Milly and Cissy woke and began crying.

It took their mother's final ounce of strength to push them along the last few yards of that epic and hazardous journey and up to the doorway of no. 25. Mill banged on the knocker to let them know she was there. She did not have the energy to pull the string from the letterbox for the key to unlock the door herself. Leaning against the wall in the porch, Mill slid to the ground completely exhausted.

"Blimey!" Mill heard her younger brother Tom call, or was it one of the others, she didn't know, the voice seemed so far off, "look what the cat's dragged in Ma!" he said calling to his mother, "It's our Mill and she's sitting on the floor!"

Many helping hands were soon seeing to the girls and helping Mill to get her wet clothes off. She shrieked in pain as they removed her boots. The boots had rubbed away the skin of her heels and were bleeding profusely. Blisters on her toes were about to burst. Her hands were stinging from the cold.

"I reckon yer've got chilblains there me girl".... Sarah her mother observed as one of the girls placed a mug of hot milk in Mill's hands.

"Blimey Mill, yer ain't walked all the way from Bethnal Green 'ave yer"?

"Yes" was all she had the strength to whisper. By now she had been wrapped in warm blankets and was sitting near the fire. She could say no more. Mill was fast asleep.

Three hours passed before the sound of the fire being raked awoke her. She opened her eyes and saw her mother opposite, dressed as always in black and sitting on an old upright wooden chair. For a minute, Mill thought of her likeness to the late Queen Victoria.

Sarah wasn't yet fifty, but looked much older than her years. Constant childbirth had certainly taken its toll on her looks and her figure.

Mill didn't quite know what sort of reception she would receive from her and had swallowed her pride because she had nowhere else to go.

"Where's me girls mum, are they all right?"

"Of course they are" her mother replied rather frostily, "they're upstairs with some of the others".

"Thank you" Mill replied.

Sarah, having not seen little Cissy before remarked how alike they both looked and then asked why Mill had arrived so unexpectedly, especially at this time of year and in such terrible weather.

Because of her mother's disapproval when they had married, it had been easier not to visit too often, besides she had a life of her own now with Jesse and their children.

'Well, at least I did have,' she thought as she began to tell them all about the events of the last few days.

Sarah listened to Mill's tale of woe and the problems they'd had, what with having no money and then Jesse signing up.

"Well, I'll give 'im his due," Sarah told her as she lifted young Milly up onto her lap, "Jesse was always a worker and if he couldn't get work what chance was there for anyone?"

Mill nodded in agreement.

Young Milly was quite happy to sit on her grandmother's lap and giggled as Sarah bounced her on her knee.

"Yer father's been called up being he's in the reserves. He went overseas when yer was just a lit'len yer know an' did 'is bit, that was the Boar War"

'Did 'is bit here as well', Mill thought looking around at the large brood of siblings.

"How long has he been gone?" she asked noticing her mother wasn't showing any signs of pregnancy.

"Six months back, when it all started, 'ere give Billy 'is bottle will yer?" Billy was Mill's youngest brother but he was only a couple of weeks younger than her own daughter, young Milly.

It was obviously there wouldn't be another mouth to feed in the very near future and Mill hoped for her mother's sake that Billy would be the last. She was quite pleased at the prospect of not seeing her father for some time and although she wouldn't say it, she suspected her mother was having the same thoughts.

"Joe's gone as well!" piped up Elsie who was Mill's eight-year-old sister.

Joe was Mill's eldest brother, being just a couple of years younger than she was.

"What did he want to go and do that for?"

"I don't know" replied her mother thoughtfully, "he just went 'nd signed up a couple of days after yer father went. Suppose he thought he'd follow 'is ol' man".

When Mill said she'd have to find somewhere to rent, it was suggested that she should go round and see old Mr Macleod who her father had been working for in Glen Road.

"He knows everyfing that goes on around 'ere what with all that building work he does, maybe he can 'elp? You'd better git around there tomorrow Mill, now- a- days places are going like 'ot cakes, seems like everyone wants to live 'ere"

"What about me stuff? I must get it tomorrow! I'll need to rent a cart"

One of the boys was sent along to see old Mr Bailey who owned the stables nearby and it was arranged for him and a lad to collect her stuff the following morning providing the weather wasn't too bad. He also agreed to her storing it in one of his empty stables. She hoped it wouldn't be snowing and the horse could manage the sludge.

The kindly old gent at the stables having known the Herod family for many years agreed to being paid when Mill received her Army Allowance which she would soon be drawing weekly. She'd have to go to the local Post office to see if she could draw her allowance from there.

That night she slept in an armchair near the fire and cribs were found for her daughters. With so many children living in the household, it didn't seem to make any difference having three more under the roof. Besides with her father and eldest brother both away in the Army there would be a bit more breathing space in the household. She'd go and see Mr Macleod and hopefully her and the girls would soon be gone anyway. She'd go first thing in the morning.

"You'll find every thing packed!" Mill called to Mr. Bailey and his lad the following morning as the cart pulled up outside. "It's all ready!"

Before leaving Gratton Houses, Mill had used her sheets to tie everything in bundles; her crockery and a few kitchen utensils; towels, blankets and clothing that hadn't been sold.

With her feet heavily bandaged after the result of her long walk the day before, she hobbled to the kerbside wearing an old pair of her mother's boots. She gave Mr. Bailey the key for Gratton House and notes she had written for Hetty and Mrs Johnson. She was pleased to see the two horses harnessed to a covered wagon. At least all her belongings would be dry when they were brought back later in the day.

"There's just the bed, Milly's cot, the table and chairs and the two fireside chairs, oh yes, and some stuff I've bundled up"

She hobbled back and stood on the doorstep. 'Was there anything else?' she wondered and thought for a moment, the curtains she'd taken down were in one of the bundles. 'What else was there?' she thought.

"Oh yes!" she cried, "Don't forget the fire guard and there's the clothes horse as well!"

"We'll just put every fing in what we see," Mr. Bailey assured her as the cart began to pull away, "Don't worry about a thing lass"

"Oh, and just shove the key through the letter box will yer when yer've done"

Thankfully it wasn't snowing but the roads were still wet with slush.

"The old gent touched his cap and then jerking the reins, was off and on their way to Bethnal Green.

She knew the Landlord would have a spare key and once the rent knocker realised they had gone he'd soon have the door opened up again and rent the place out to someone else.

When Mr Macleod heard of Mill's plight and being her father was still officially employed by his company, he suggested a house that was available just around the corner in Netley Road and as luck had it, he was the owner.

"A house! Do you mean the whole house?" She was flabbergasted.

"Yeah, well I was going to let it out in rooms but I ain't got time to sort it all out, it's yours if yer want it girl. I 'ad to chuck the last tenants out, they got behind with the rent, but it will only be 'til the war's over 'cos then I'm selling up" She was absolutely delighted at the prospects of renting a whole house and couldn't wait to get back to tell her mother"

"He's letting me have it really cheap being dad's been a good worker and both 'im, Joe an' Jesse are out in France dong their bit for the country.

"Bloody 'ell Mill, 'cor that's a turn up for the books, 'ow yer going to furnish it? Those 'ouses round there have got three bedrooms"

"Wouldn't it be better for you and our lot Mum to find a house like that? Crickey, with all of you living in this small place you could certainly do with more room"

"Nah, I like it 'ere 'an the only way I'll ever leave 'ere is in me box"

Her words were to come true, she never did move from that house but it would not be for another thirty eight years that they carried her out, in a box even though it was a coffin.

Two days later Mill and the girls were in a nice terraced house with three bedrooms upstairs, a front parlour downstairs that had a lovely bay window, a back room, a scullery and the usual outside lavatory. And there was even a small garden! The girls would love that as they got older and oh, just wait until she wrote to Jesse! If it hadn't been for him joining up goodness knows where they would have ended up...possibly in the Workhouse. She shuddered at the thought.

The previous tenants had by chance left a couple of buckets of coal and she decided it would be better for now if they just lived in the back room until she could get some more furniture and make a nice home for them all.

Her mother seemed to have forgotten her disapproval of when she'd left home to marry Jesse and told her to come round and eat with the family until she could draw her money and get settled in. Knowing how hard Sarah was struggling herself Mill was very grateful for this offer.

It was hard to believe that so much had happened in the space of one week and hoped she didn't wake up to find she'd dreamed it all. She and Jesse had never been parted before and being in a strange house without him she felt a bit nervous but she'd soon get used to that. They had a lovely new home, how wonderful it would be for him when he got back and hopefully if her mother looked after the girls she might be able to get a job of some sorts and would then be able to afford some odd bits and pieces to furnish it. She was glad that she had bundled up her heavy side curtains and not left them hanging back at Gratton Houses and she had Jesse's letter to look forward to and would eagerly await its arrival via her mother's house. She could then reply and tell him where they were now living and all about the events of the last week.

She had made the back room as comfortable as she could and there was now a fire burning in the grate thanks to the previous tenants. She'd have to look out for the coalman. She wasn't too far from Walthamstow High Street and the market so she'd probably be able to get some cheap vegetables to make broth or maybe a bit of scraggy end from a butcher to boil up with them. Yes, wait 'til Jesse got back, everything was going to be fine.

She went into the empty front parlour and looked out of the window onto her new neighbourhood. It wasn't really all that different from Globe Road, except the houses were bigger than those opposite the dwellings and the weather was certainly the same. There was no getting away from that.

'Well Jesse' she said softly to herself turning from the window, 'I know where I am, but where on earth are you?'

Now that she had time to reflect back over the events of the last few days, Mill suddenly knew as the tears began to stream down her face what a wonderfully brave man her husband was.

He had tried to convince her that this terrible war would soon come to an end and he may not even have to go to France, but in her heart she knew it could be a very long time before she saw him again. He had joined the Army so that she and their children would have food on the table and not have to rely on other people's leavings. It wasn't much for any man to ask, but what price would he be expected to pay? She covered her face with her apron and sobbed.

Chapter Five

Come June Jesse was on board ship heading for France. Things were certainly not going the way he had expected or indeed had hoped. He had been sent to Basingstoke in Hampshire shortly after his arrival at Guildford and that had taken him even further away from London and his family. He'd learnt to use a rifle and to recognise 'who was who' when it came to the higher ranks. He could now salute correctly, although there had been a few occasions where he'd thought a couple of his own signs would have been much more appropriate!

There had been the hours and hours of square bashing until the men had been drilled to march in perfect step: daily physical exercises where muscles he never even knew he had ached and on Sundays there were Church Parades where attendance was compulsory. At least he was getting some decent grub now and had even gained a bit of weight, so some good had come out of it. And the main thing was that Mill had an income so she and the girls wouldn't be going short any more.

Recently the training had been even harder. Word had gone around that many of their regiment already at the front line had suffered terrible losses. They had been attacked in the early hours of the 16th. May when twenty-one Officers out of the twenty-two stationed there had been killed. Out of seven hundred and thirty-three other ranks, four hundred and thirty-three were among the listed dead.

Reinforcements had already been sent out to replace those who had been killed, but more men were still needed and Jesse's battalion was considered ready.

That morning as they left Basingstoke for Southampton, the men had marched past Lord Kitchener as he sat on his horse and taken the salute. They were now all part of his 'New Army'; men from all walks of life who until just a short time back were ordinary men living in ordinary towns and villages. If anyone had told them, when they were celebrating Christmas with their families, that they would be serving in France by the following June, they would have fell about laughing. The idea would have been that ridiculous. Jesse looked over the side of the ship as the vessel made its way through the calm sea. He had never been on a boat before and normally the chance of doing so would have been exciting. There was no excitement in his heart now, just fear of what lay ahead. They were all on their way to France as replacements for those Tommie's who had probably been on this very same ship just a couple of months earlier and were now laying dead, the thought filled him with an icy cold fear.

They had all been given a 48-hour pass prior to be being drafted. This didn't give him a lot of time to do the return trip from Basingstoke to Walthamstow, but he had to get home to see Mill and the girls just once. The journey had been difficult and he had spent precious hours waiting for connections. When he had finally arrived at their new home in Netley Road, Mill was over the moon to see him and was so proud of the solider that now looked so fit and well. It was the first time she had seen him in uniform; he had left in his old cloth cap and overcoat and had come home smartly dressed in khaki. But the few short hours passed quickly and left him with little time to get back to Basingstoke.

Mill begged him not to leave but of course he had too, he knew the consequences if he didn't. He told her not to go with him to the station but to stay at home with the girls. He didn't want an emotional goodbye like they'd had before, that would be just too painful. This time he knew where he was heading and the thought of leaving Mill and the girls was breaking his heart but he knew he had to go. Like before he held her tight and told her he'd be back, he told her he loved her and as she stood at the gate sobbing he left. Jesse never looked back; he didn't want her to see the tears that matched her own. He quickened his step and with a heavy heart, headed for the station.

By the time he did eventually get back to barracks he had overstayed his leave by 18 hours and had to go before his Commanding Officer.

"This will go down on your record Warren and you will lose 10 days pay. Just think yourself lucky that you got back before we sailed, if not you would have been shot for desertion."

"Yes Sir!" Jesse replied. He was worried about the amount of money being docked from Mill's allowance, but it was well worth the loss of pay to see each other just once more before he went to France. As luck had it, when he checked his pay book only two days money had been docked. He didn't know why this was but he was very grateful to who ever had relented but he felt sure his Commanding Officer had something to do with it. Although Jesse would never know, his superior officer did indeed have compassion for all these young men now going to face the worst nightmare they could ever have possibly imagined.

It was a beautiful June day and Jesse rested his arms on the rail of the ship as he surveyed the tranquil scene before him. Waves lapped gently against the side as the vessel cut through the deep waters of the English Channel. Flotsam and green seaweed floated past along with a plank of driftwood possibly from some old ship long since rotted away. Jesse could see where the rusty bolts had once been held secure.

A wash of frothy white foam trailed behind the ship forming a wide wake that gradually spread across the water and slowly blended back into the sea.

He could taste the salt air and felt a slight breeze on his face. The smell of the ozone reminded him of the day he and Mill had spent at Leigh-on-Sea on the Essex coast not long after they had first met. That until now had been the only time he had ever seen the sea.

Someone said they were heading for a place called Calais, 'Where the bleeding 'ell is that?' he wondered and thought it might as well be Tim-Buck-to for all he knew.

The screech of a sea gull over head made him look up. Above the sky was clear blue with just a few puffs of white cloud. The smoke from the ships two funnels slowly followed behind like a long trailing grey ribbon gradually disappearing into the distant haze.

For a few moments he closed his eyes and thought how Mill would have liked to see all this, and then the sound of someone retching nearby brought him back to reality.

A chap was leaning over the side being sick, as were several others. Jesse looked around at his companions, he had got to know a few of the men well and felt the comradeship the whole battalion shared. They were all in it together now and knew they would soon stand together in the trenches. It was inevitable that many would die together too. Jesse was well aware of this fact and wondered if he would ever cross these waters again. There would be no return trip home for dead soldiers.

Whereas Jesse had seen the sea before, being just the once, the majority of these men never had, let alone sailed to foreign climes and as the ship docked many were at the ships rails trying to get a glimpse of the French countryside.

"Don't look much different to back home, does it?" said a chap standing next to him. Jesse noticed that like himself he too was a private.

"Suppose not," he replied, but then he'd only been outside London the once when he had gone on the train with Mill to Leigh on Sea. He recalled there had been plenty of green fields as they'd looked from the windows of the train so he guessed France must be like the English countryside.

"It's certainly different from what I'm used to, I've lived in the Smoke all me life".

None of the men had any idea where they were heading and after disembarking from the ship they began a march that lasted two hours.

They came to a huge field just outside a small town that was to be their headquarters for the next few months. Hundreds of white bell shaped tents in long rows had been erected and many appeared to be already occupied.

Many of the men were exhausted, their boots had rubbed away the skin on their heels and feet and those who had been ill on the ship looked in a sorry state.

"Right!", barked their Commanding Officer, "twenty men to a tent and I want you all back here in fifteen minutes. Go!"

The ship load of men who had gratefully fallen to the ground for a few minutes rest pulled themselves up and made a move to find a sleeping area. Jesse who couldn't wait to get his boots off found himself in a tent near to the latrines. He knew he was there because of the smell.

'Oh, well' he thought, 'might be handy in the night'

"Christ!" Jesse said aloud as he entered the tent, "How the hell do we get twenty in 'ere?" Back at Basingstoke there had only been six to a tent.

Bedding rolls were laid out with the foot of each one forming a circle around the centre pole in the middle. Jesse went for a space near the door, even sleeping near the latrines would be better than being in the middle of that lot.

Twenty minutes later they all stood to attention while their platoon Sergeants briefed them. In the distance thunder could be heard, or so most of them thought.

"If you think there's a storm brewing", bawled the Sergeant, "then you're right!" he paused for a moment," but it ain't what you think! It's the Jerries shelling ours boys and that's were you'll all be by tomorrow evening!! We're about four miles from the Front Line" he told them.

Jesse felt sick in his stomach, the Sergeant went on,

"There will be no deserters" he was saying, "and we don't want any cowards here either. The penalty for these offences is the firing squad! And for those of you who don't believe me, I have a list of names to read out to you!"

Reading from the sheet he held in front of him, he began calling out several names and ages of men who had been shot for desertion and cowardice in the last two weeks. Jesse could not believe his ears…"19 years old ….20 years old….. 22 years old… 18 years old". These lads were younger than he was!

He thought of the day he'd joined up and the Sergeant at the desk had told the youngster in front of him to 'come back in the afternoon when he was older'. And then there was the mother who came looking for her sixteen-year-old son. How many of these lads who had faced the firing squad were under age? How many had wished that their mother's had come looking for them? What a terrible wicked waste of life,

"The bastards" Jesse muttered under his breath.

"Something to say Warren!" yelled the Sergeant.

"No…Sir!"

"Right!" the Sergeant was bellowing again, "you have until noon tomorrow to do as you please, there's grub being got ready over there," he told them indicating towards the field kitchen, " and if you do go into town, we don't want any trouble or shacking up with any women."

A murmur and a few chuckles went around. The Sergeant hadn't finished,

"We ain't spent all this time and money training you lot to come out here and start off with a bleeding dose of the clap! You'll be court marshalled if you end up with it and it might be your name I'm reading out next!" he bellowed

The men got the message.

Jesse decided to opt out on the offer of food, his stomach wouldn't take it. He was terrified at the thought of knowing that the following day he would be heading for the front line.

He decided to walk the short distance into the town, maybe there was a Tavern there. No-one had said anything about not having a drink and he certainly needed something to help calm his nerves.

The buildings were different from back home; most had windows that were long and narrow with white wooden shutters either side. The doors were painted in various colours and window boxes, although mostly empty of plants, sat on the window ledges.

It was quite busy, soldiers from various units were standing about in groups talking and Jesse noticed for the first time in his life, men wearing skirts, although he recalled Mill once telling him that Scotsmen wear kilts, nor skirts. It was all the same to him, kilts or skirts and it amused him to see them dressed in this manner and wondered if there was any truth in what he'd heard and maybe they didn't wear any undergarments? They were all big burley men from the Highland Regiments and as curious as he was, he certainly had no intentions of finding out,

The place was bigger than Jesse had first thought and there were a variety of shops although mostly closed. Jesse tried to read the French names; Boulangerie; Boucherie and Pharmacie were among them.

He was pleased to see a crowd of uniformed men standing outside a building with beer tankards in their hands and he guessed this must be a tavern of sorts. He had heard that the French only drank wine but they might have beer although anything with a drop of alcohol in it would go down really well despite the fear that was churning his stomach over.

Making his way towards the Tavern Jesse heard a voice behind him,

"Well stone the crows! If it ain't Jesse Warren!".

Turning Jesse a found a familiar face looking at him,

"Well, cor blimey, George East, fancy seeing you 'ere!"

It was a chap he had known from Bethnal Green who had been in the trade like Jesse. He was a cabinetmaker and had a small business off Cambridge Heath Road. Jesse had polished some of George's work and the two had got to know each other pretty well.

They shook hands and thumped each other on the shoulders,

"So they got you as well Jesse, when did you join up?

"February", he paused and then added, "Still can't believe I'm bloody well 'ere ".

"Yeah, I know how yer feel mate, I'm a Sapper now with the Royal Engineers. I'm in with the 525th Reserve Field Company."

The two East Enders pleased that by chance they had met up so many miles from home, went off together towards the tavern. They had a lot of catching up to do and talked about life back in Bethnal Green and made a few feeble jokes although both knew the terror and apprehension the other must have been feeling.

After a couple of rather warm beers George suggested they had their photographs taken.

"There's some bloke got a little shop round the corner from 'ere. He puts the picture on a post card and he's doing a roaring trade. And he only charges a tanner" (6d-2.5 p)

"No way!" Jesse laughed, "I've never had me picture taken in me life, not even when I got married".

"Well how about having it done for yer missus then, she'd love that an' you can post it to 'er with a message on the back".

Jesse gave it some thought especially when he remembered it would be Mill's birthday in about three weeks, "Well I suppose I could send it as a birthday present, couldn't I? Yeah, alright then, I'll give it a go"

"Come on then mate," George said leading the way to where a queue was lining up outside a little shop.

Both men were glad of each other's company and chatted while they waited. Jesse was surprised to hear that George's wife Charlotte had also packed up and gone to live in Walthamstow.

"I reckon half of Bethnal Green must be moving over there" he said, "What road is your missus living in then?" Jesse asked wondering if it was anywhere near Mill.

George told him she was in St. John's Road, on the boarders of Walthamstow and Chingford but Jesse wasn't familiar with that area. He did however recall that his mother had been buried over that way at Chingford Mount Cemetery when he was just a young lad.

"How many lit'lens yer got now George? It was two girls last time I saw yer"

"Got three now, all girls"

"I've got two girls me self now, funny fing is, I met some chap when I was signing on, he 'ad loads of girls in 'is family, must be something in the water at Bethnal Green"

George laughed, "Or the beer!"

The sounds of the distant guns seemed to be louder, Jesse was beginning to wish he hadn't drunk the beer. He face must have showed how he was feeling,

"It's alright mate, I feel the same".

George was taller than Jesse, in fact Jesse felt everyone was taller than him but he felt comfort as George put his arm around his shoulder and said,

"Come on mate, we'll be alright, you wait and see, we'll get through it." and with a slap on Jesse's back cried, "Come on you ugly sod, lets see if we can crack the camera!"

They agreed to meet up again the following morning to collect their photographs before they left for the front. This didn't help one bit to take Jesse's mind off what lie ahead, he was feeling sick and terrified but it would be a good to see George's familiar face again and a chance for a bit of banter and talk of home before they parted.

Orders had been given, 'Be prepared to leave at 12 noon for the march to the front line'.

George was waiting as arranged and after a couple of handshakes and thumping each other on the shoulders they went off together to collect the photographs.

There was George with a big smile on his face and then there was Jesse looking as scared as hell. Even he could see the fear in own eyes.

"I can't send her that! I look petrified"

"Guess we're all scared stiff Jesse, just a bit of a fluke that I was smiling when I had mine done"

"No, I ain't sending it"

" 'Course yer can" replied his mate, who had just finished writing on the back of his, "Here, borrow me pencil"

George asked Jesse if he would put his picture postcard for Charlotte in the postbag as he had to get back to his regiment, they were leaving before Jesse's lot.

He was happy to do so and the two mates said their farewells.

"Let's 'ope we all make it back 'ome an' get back to normal when this bloody lot's all over, it's been really great seeing yer George".

"Yeah, you too mate, look after yerself and keep yer 'ead down; we'll have a pint when we get back home".

"Well, with my height or lack of it I'll be alright there, no need to keep me 'ead down" he replied jokingly.

"Yeah, Good luck mate, see yer back in the Smoke"

George gave a wave and went on his way.

Jesse sat on a wall and looked again at his own photograph and thought he might as well send it since he'd had it done. Turning it over he saw printed on the back 'Carte' and below this 'Correspondence.'

He then realised he still had George's pencil,

'Oh, well' he thought, 'I'll hang on to it 'til I see 'im sometime' then he tried to think of something to say to Mill.

He sat for a while and then wrote his message;

My Dear Mill, What do you think of this. I am not crying but nearly by the look of me. I will send a letter as soon as we settle. We are on the move again getting near the front. All my love, from Jesse.

Jesse wasn't to know that he would never see George East again. George was invalided out of the Army after being gassed while on active service in the trenches. Sadly he died on 15th March 1917 from the effects of the poisonous gas. He left a wife Charlotte and three young daughters; Emily, Lucy and Charlotte. Many, many, years later his grandson Paul White, (son of Emily) married Pamela Seager who became a great friend of the author.

The following day after a four-mile march, Jesse and his comrades were at the front line. They had no idea what the Battlefields would look like or the 'no man's land' that separated them for the enemy. None of them had any previous Military experience apart from the brief training over the recent weeks. They were all volunteers like Jesse and like Jesse they were scared and wondered what the hell they were doing there.

Jesse jumped down into the trench following the others, "File along", their Sergeant barked, "Spread yourselves along and make yourselves comfy lads. Might as well make yourselves at home, you'll be living here for the next three weeks!"

"Where do we sleep then Sarge?" one of the privates asked.

"Well we ain't got any feather beds 'ere son, find yourself a space an' call it home".

Before anyone else could utter another word, a loud explosion shook the ground and frightened the living daylights out of all of them. A shell exploded within yards of the trench throwing earth and rubble high into the air, which rained down on the men. Jesse threw himself against the side of the trench and now knew why they had been given an order to wear their helmets. His heart was thumping.

"Christ Almighty!" someone said, "What the hell was that?"

No one had been seriously hurt, apart from a few cuts and bruising, but most of them were shaken up. They were given the order to stand on the step that ran along the trench and prepare to fire. Almost immediately another shell exploded, this time sending shrapnel into the trench along with more falling earth. Jesse ducked and tried to protect himself with his arms over his head and it was then that he heard the most agonising scream….. A chap about his own age had been hit, a large slice of metal was embedded in his chest and blood was spurting from the wound like a fountain. Blood was oozing from his mouth and nose and Jesse knew as the poor sod fell to the ground that he was dead. A deep gash had almost severed an arm exposing flesh and bone was running with blood. Just ten minutes into the trenches and already the first life had been taken.

The Sergeant called for stretcher-bearers and as the unfortunate lad was taken away, several men, including Jesse, were retching their guts out like never before.

And so began life in the trenches. The long days became long weeks and death was always with them. The screams of injured men and cries of the dying filled his head. At first Jesse was terrified but as time passed his fear turned to anger as he saw the men who he had trained and drunk with being blown to pieces. He knew each day could be his last day too and always marvelled at the fact that he was still alive. Slowly the long weeks ran into long months and the anger Jesse held in his heart turned to acceptance. He knew there was nothing he could do and the war would go on until the stupidity of it all came to an end. No one knew when that that would be or how it would all end, but he had to accept the inevitable facts to keep his own sanity. Not only was the war taking the lives of so many men, but also the minds of those still living.

On one occasion Jesse came across a man, probably in his mid thirties, sitting huddled in one the holes dug into the side of the trench for protection.

"You aright mate?" he asked.

The solider, a big built man, was shaking and crying,

"I can't find me way 'ome", came the pitiful reply as he began to rock backwards and forwards and then asked Jesse if he had seen his dog.

This was no joke, the man really did believe he was lost and his dog had gone missing too.

"Sal! Sal!" he began calling, "Where are you girl?"

"Come on mate, pull yourself together" Jesse said sympathetically but it was no use. The man's mind could take no more of the abominable terrors that surrounded him. Jesse went in search of a medic.

During the following months Jesse prayed every night that this living nightmare would come to an end and every night he thought of Mill and the girls and prayed that one day he'd be home. He could never have imagined the indescribable carnage that lay in the fields of France and Flanders. If he was lucky enough to survive all this and lived to be a hundred years old he would never ever forget the repulsion and horrors of this hell on earth.

Here he was, a French Polisher from the East End of London marching through the Mennen Gates at Ypres to fight in fields of mud that often came up to his waist. He saw men slip from the duck boards used to cross this wet sodden mire and slowly disappear below, too weak from exhaustion to help themselves. Thousands and thousands died this way as the rain fell for days on end turning the fields into graves for those still living. There was no way anyone could help them, the weight of their packs took them down and men still lying on boards hadn't the strength to pull the unfortunate ones free. Some offered their rifles, but the grip was soon lost as wet muddy hands slipped further away.

The more it rained the deeper the mud became; even horses were seen to disappear and sometimes if they were lucky, a quick bullet brought their struggling to a swift end. But how could you shoot a comrade, who begged and cried out,

"Shoot me! Shoot me! For God's sake shoot me!" as he was slowly being sucked down and under. Firing at the enemy was one thing, but to shoot one of your own would take courage beyond belief. Jesse hoped that there was someone blessed with the special strength to help a fellow comrade.

Still they were urged to go on, caked in heavy mud and boots that hadn't been removed for three weeks or more. Trench foot soon followed and many were hesitant to remove their boots in fear of their toes having rotted. Rations and fresh water was often delayed and all around lay the dead. Bodies could lie for days where they had fallen and the sight of rotting limbs and flesh that had been torn apart by the constant shelling was now common place.

Jesse was one of the lucky ones who came back through the Mennen Gate when thousands of his fellow men never would. But even after a few short days rest he was marched back to France and still it went on and on. Then came the winter with it's icy conditions and snow, men were in agony with frostbite and trench foot. Many were sent to the field hospital for treatment only to come back when the condition improved. Sometimes after a short sleep Jesse would awake and be amazed to find he was still alive and thought it a miracle that he was still amongst the living. He soon learnt that every day he survived was like an added bonus to his life. None of them knew who would be next, they just prayed it wouldn't be them, but so many prayers weren't being answered in this living hell.

Among the living, and the dead, was another terrifying horror something they all feared ….the rats. They would come out at night, sometimes hundreds of them scurrying along the top of the trenches against the night sky. The smell of death hanging in the air always attracted them and on a quiet night they would scamper down the walls to scavenge amongst the sleeping men. Some men would rather face the Germans than wake up to see a rodent inches from their face, they could live with the dead but they dreaded the rats.

The lack of bathing facilities and wearing the same clothing for weeks on end bought another loathsome parasite to the trenches and the men carried them everywhere. Lice…in their uniforms, lice in their hair and beards and worst of all, in the unwashed underwear. These creatures dug into the skin and attached themselves to the most delicate parts of the flesh where many a man already had sores or boils from the chaffing of soiled clothing. The only way they could keep the numbers down was to remove the infested garments and run a lighted candle along the seams which was the favourite place for breeding. But within hours they were back again and men still went into battle often filthy dirty, sometimes hungry, alive with lice, suffering painful sores and other discomforts.

When the call came to go 'Over the top!' they had one of two choices; face the enemy with the possibility of a certain death or face a firing squad for cowardice.

Some men did meet their death the latter way, not because they were cowards but because they froze with fear at the atrocities and horrific sights that befell their eyes. Some were so bewildered and shocked that they couldn't speak, let alone move. Even when they were in front of a firing squad they didn't know what was happening. Some were Regulars that had been out there since the war began and many were just ordinary every day run of the mill blokes like himself who had volunteered. Jesse found it hard to believe that his own country could call them cowards and execute them because their minds and bodies just couldn't take any more.

How he kept going he never knew. He often thought, as the shelling and bombing was hitting the ground around him, sometimes bullets missing him by inches, of Mill and the girls' back home. He remembered the day when he'd joined up and how he stood looking along Globe Road as the coal man called out, 'Coals for cash!'

He remembered how cold he had been that morning and how the wet slush had seeped through a hole in his boot. That had been sheer Heaven compared to what life was like now and he longed to be back home. He never dreamed that he would be spending his twenty- fifth birthday digging with a party of seven officers and 385 N.C.O's constructing a firing position in the trenches, let alone fighting in a war.

One day the order to advance had been given and Jesse was in the midst of the firing. Shells were blasting and machine gun fire was ripping the ground around him. Earth was raining down as he ran forward holding his rifle before him. The noise was ear shattering, smoke and dust obscured his vision. A shell landed nearby and exploded throwing Jesse to the ground. Several bodies lay near where he had fallen, some ripped to pieces spreading dismembered limbs and torn flesh over the churned up ground. Around him men cried for help and the screams of others thrown into the tangle of barbed wire were soon silenced by the German's guns.

For several minutes Jesse kept his head down and his face to the ground. Close by he heard the groaning of an injured man, he turned his head to see another chap was cradling a very badly injured man in his arms and crying,

"Come on Charlie, oh, come on! You've got to make it, you've got to make it! Oh, God!" he cried out, "He's my brother, he's my brother!"

It was obvious that the injured man wasn't going anywhere. A huge expanse of flesh protruded where his left arm had once been. Both men were covered in blood.

The badly mutilated man opened his eyes and Jesse heard him say to his brother,

"Don't let mother see me like this Tom, don't let her see me."

"She won't see you Charlie, she won't see you, our mum's dead" sobbed his brother.

"Tell her to go back, make her go back"

With his last ounce of strength the dying man lifted his head and cried, "Look Tom, she's there behind you, mum's standing behind you, make her go back, mum go back! Please Tom make.....".

Suddenly an almighty roar went over Jesse's head as a shell passed where he could have easily been standing. The ground shook as it landed several yards behind him.

He kept his head down and waited for the debris to settle. "Christ! That was bloody close!" But he was still alive!

Apart from a load of earth that had partially covered him he was O.K. The two brothers were nowhere to be seen. Darkened blood and fragments of flesh were all that remained.

Jesse took some comfort from the thought that the dying man had seen his mother as his life was taken from him. Did the other brother see her as well in those split seconds before death had claimed them both?

Jesse wondered if he would see his own mother when his turn came because he felt sure it would. How could his luck hold out? There were so many dying around him; he knew the next shell could have his name on it. Would Mary Ann come for him, like the mother who had come for her two boys? Jesse thought how nice it would be to see his mother and to see Mill and the girls. His head was aching and he felt very, very tired. Several other bodies lay around him, some dismembered and there were men screaming in agony. He couldn't move to help them, he wanted to but darkness was engulfing him, 'Just need to sleep' he thought, 'just need to sleep'. "Mill, where are you me darling?" he heard a voice calling out not realising it was his own as he drifted into unconsciousness.

A boot hitting him the ribs suddenly bought him back to his senses and he yelled out in pain.

"Oh, Christ, sorry mate!" he heard a voice call as someone tripped over him, "I thought you were a gonna".

"Well, I bloody well ain't but I might just as well be!" Jesse retorted, "What's going on?"

The shelling had ceased and just a few rounds of fire could be heard.

"Dunno, but the orders are to head back". Jesse didn't know how long he'd been there and kicked off the earth that had fallen onto his legs and chest, pulled himself up and followed the others heading back. Medics were trying to help those who were barely alive and stretcher-bearers were carrying the wounded back to the trenches. Although now hardened to the sights, sounds and smell of death, trying to walk over those who hadn't made it and the remains of what had once been men was enough to make any man lose his mind; would he know if he'd gone mad? Would they shoot him for it? How much longer could they go on for? He uttered several oaths and thought of all the families back home who would never know that their men folk had died in this unimaginable and atrocious way. Killed in Action, sounded like a heroic way to die but for many it would never reveal the real horror and true facts that lay behind that account. More shells began firing and Jesse threw himself to the ground as they all did. There would be many who never got up again. "Poor buggers" he uttered sadly.

Every three weeks or so the exhausted men were relieved by another battalion and then returned to their billets for a few days of rest and recuperation. Their first thoughts were a bath, a change of clothes and a real decent meal followed hopefully, by a long undisturbed sleep

Jesse had often seen men on a route march or when in battle collapse without showing any signs of injury. For some it was fatigue but for other's it was much worst. Completely drained of all energy their bodies and souls could take no more. Their hearts just gave out and as they fell, they died.

Once rested and cleaned up the able bodied had a few days to unwind and recover their physical and hopefully their mental strength before returning back to the trenches. Occasionally there would be some form of distraction that would be a welcome relief and help take their minds away from the thoughts of returning to the battlefields.

Once when Jesse had only been in France a few weeks, their regimental band played and they all cheered as Sgt. Dr. Forman came forward as the conductor, but no one had heard the band play since. He thought that probably half of them had copped it by now.

Before they were on the march again they had bathed in the river Ancre near Ville. Musketry practice and physical training followed, but the chance of swimming in the river was absolute bliss.

A couple of days later as they marched through Picquigny to new billets at St. Sauveur, the whole Battalion were filmed when a cinematographer sent from the War Office came to film the troops. Most of them had never seen a camera that actually took moving pictures before so they all waved and raised their hats as they passed by. There was a lot laughing in the ranks as they joked about being film stars and who had the better looks. Sadly, many of these gallant men would never get the chance of seeing them-selves marching on a giant silver screen at some picture palace back home. The war would see to that, taking with it every dream these men ever had for the future. They had to live one day at time, never knowing whether or not it would be their last and if a diversion came along that could give them a bit of entertainment, they took full advantage of it. This is where Jesse came in; for months now he'd had his own method of entertaining the troops and it was something well to his advantage when it came to making a profit.

During his training period at Southampton, he'd had the opportunity to purchase a Crown and Anchor board for just a few pence from an old solider since retired and in ill health. Jesse had seen this game being played outside many a pub or down some alleyway when he was a lad and knew all the methods of fleecing a punter. It was meant to be a game of chance, but it was also an illegal form of gambling banned in Public Houses as well as in the Army. It was the way the 'Banker' always turned the tables to his own advantage that caused trouble and even Jesse was no exception and had a very good system of making sure the majority of money staked out ended up own his own pocket.

The idea of the game was for the 'Banker' who of course was always Jesse, to throw a dice decorated with pictures of crowns and anchors onto the board. The punter would have to call 'Crown!' or 'Anchor!' as the dice was thrown and would win if his 'call' landed on a corresponding square. Whether or not it was skill on Jesse's part or the dice was weighted it's not known but he knew how to persuade a gullible punter they were on a winning streak. For a couple of pennies he would get a young Private to keep a lookout for any approaching Officers and then when the punter thought he was on a good thing Jesse encouraged him to raise the stakes. When there was a good amount of cash being laid down, the lookout, after getting a pre arranged signal from Jesse, would suddenly rush over crying,

"Quick! Quick everyone scarper! Some-one's coming!"

Jesse being ready for this would quickly slam the board shut, slide the money into his hat and run. If the punter did ever catch up with him, Jesse would say the dice had landed unlucky and the unfortunate solider had lost his money. This is why the game caused so much trouble.

However, Jesse nearly did come a cropper once when one of the chaps who'd been done out of a large sum of money came up behind him and gave him a whispered warning,

"I'll get even with you mate", he said with a vengeance, "just have eyes in the back of your head, 'cause you don't know when it'll be."

This worried Jesse, he'd got through this bloody war so far without being blown up or getting a bullet from the Germans. He'd been real lucky and wanted to keep it that way and didn't fancy being done over by someone on his own side. There was only twenty-four hours before they marched back and as they both came from different regiments it would be very unlikely they would meet up again once they had left the town. Meanwhile he needed some protection and thought of a plan.

The town where they were they were resting was Bray-sur-Somme in the Somme Valley. There were also several other platoons from various regiments billeted there. Those who were lucky had been allocated rooms with the local residents and Jesse was one of them. He and a couple of men from the 'Queen's' had been sharing a room in a small house next to where men from a Highland Regiment were billeted. Jesse thought he'd have a word with one of them.

He walked back towards the house being very wary of anyone following him,

'So far, so good' he thought as he turned the corner into the street where he was kipping down. He noticed one of the Scottish soldiers leaning against the window ledge having a smoke. Jesse went up to him and made some small talk and after a while asked the Scott if he was interested in earning a bit of spare cash. It will only be for a couple of days he'd told but I could use your help

The man stood up and stretched himself to his full height, which was about six foot three and looked down at Jesse.

"Aye, but it depends on what I have to do," he replied in his strong Scots accent. I'll no be doing anything illegal laddie"

Jesse explained the situation and the soldier gave it some though and then asked how much he was willing to pay.

Jesse wasn't keen to pay out too much and offered 6d (2.5 p) which would be the equivalent to half a days pay.

Just then another chap from a different regiment came over to join them. It was obvious that the two men knew each other and his height met that of the Scot, who told him about Jesse's proposition,

"Tell you what" said the second solider, "Count me in and we'll do it for 9d (approx. 4p)."

Jesse thought he was being taken for a ride, but he did have a nice sum of money tucked away in his inside pocket and although it meant forking out more than he anticipated, there was after all safety in numbers. He agreed with them and they struck a deal. They would be behind him at all times when he was outside on his own and when a game was in play. This gave Jesse a great sense of relief and a feeling of security so now he didn't have to worry about being done over.

Just then a photographer was seen going along the street trying to persuade men in uniform to have their photographs taken. The Scot who had introduced himself as James MacDonald was keen on the idea.

"Blimey," Jesse said laughing as he looked up at the two giants who were now his 'minders', "if I send one 'ome to me Missus with you two in it she'll think I've shrunk!"

A few men were having photographs taken in groups and fooling around. A chap Jesse knew from his own lot went into the house and came out with a chair,

"Here Jesse!" he called out, "stand on this!"

"Are you taking the piss?" Jesse said pretending to be serious," 'cause if yer are, I'll set me men on yer".

A lot of banter went on and then for the fun of it Jesse got up on the chair. The men thought it hilarious as he was only just slightly above the two strapping soldiers standing either side of him.

"Why don't you take the chair back with you to the trenches!" someone called out, "you'll be able to see over the top then!"

There was a lot of laughter,

"What and get me bleeding head blown off" Jesse quipped, "not so bloody likely!"

"Well you can always have a sit down and read your Sunday paper while you're waiting for the Hun!" piped up another.

The relaxed atmosphere was a great booster for the men and laughter was a real tonic. They all knew they would be going back to the trenches soon and many had spent a few hours writing to their loved ones back home and wondering if it would be the last letter they would ever write. A bit of fun was just what they needed and it relieved the pressures and tension that threatened to drive them all insane.

After a lot of clowning around Jesse got off the chair and sat down.

"Right, come on, let's be serious", he said although still laughing himself, "If I'm having me picture taken with you two, then I'll rather sit down, at least I won't look like a little short arse!"

Suddenly he had second thoughts, "Come to think of it, I don't really fancy the idea of having it done at all," he said as he went to get up.

His two 'Minder's' stood to the back of him, the Scot was to his left and the other chap said,

"Sit down man and let's get it done" as he put his hand on Jesse's shoulder. Whether it was to retain him or just a friendly gesture, Jesse wasn't too sure, but before he could get up again the photographer who had disappeared under a black cloth, called out, "Right hold it....... smile!" and as he came out from under the cover said "That will be 6d each please in British coins".

"When do we get our pictures then?" Jesse asked.

"I'll have them ready for you in the morning," said the photographer handing out his cards.

"Well I'll pay yer when I collect". Jesse told him. He was wise to these tricks. He'd once heard of someone in the Smoke doing a photo scam near the Tower of London. Apparently some bloke had been taking pictures of tourists without plates in his camera and then doing a disappearing act with the money.

Jesse thought at the time what a nice little earner someone had got themselves'.

Jesse with his two 'Minders'. W.W.1, France.

Jesse above and George East

'He liked to hear of a bit of enterprise, after all he was doing well with the Crown & Anchor board, but no one was going to pull a fast one on him, he was too clever for that.

So it was agreed that he would pay for the picture in the morning.

Christ!' he thought as he put the card in his tunic pocket, 'just as well I haven't paid for it, 'cos we could all be blown sky high during the night'.

He could hear the sound of the gunfire in the distance and wondered how many pictures were never collected,

"Poor sods", he said to himself as they all made their way to the local Tavern. It would be the last chance of a beer before the march back to the trenches the following day and for many it would be their last drink ever. It wasn't that he was full of gloom and doom or being pessimistic, it was just how things were and they all knew it. They were just thankful when they lived for another day.

There weren't many that didn't have this thought in the back of their minds when they raised their tankards and wished each other, "All the best!" and "Bottoms up!"

Jesse collected his picture the following day and shook hands with his two 'Minders' whom he never saw ever again.

It was time to leave Bray and head back for the trenches where they were going to relieve the 22nd. Manchester's and head for a trench known as the 'Rat-Hole' at the Minden Post. There was a lot of activity when they got there and during the early hours of the following morning they were heavily bombarded. The enemy actually raided the trenches and during the fighting took several men prisoners. The rest of the men 'stood to' waiting for further action after this, but there was no more that night. At roll call, it was noted that ten men were missing, not including several who lay dead.

Later during a quiet moment when the firing had ceased, Jesse sat in the trench and read the last letter he had received from Mill, which had been a couple of month's back. It was now dirty and dog eared and had got wet but he would keep it until it fell apart. She and the children were well and she had got herself a part time job doing machine work in a local factory. Mill was pleased to tell him that her mother was actually looking after the children and it seemed that at last she had forgiven them for getting married!

The letter went on to say that she had been over to Bethnal Green and seen Hetty Samuels and Mrs Johnson. Young Billy had married and was now in the Army himself. All Hetty knew about John was that he was somewhere in France.

'Well at least there's been no telegram' he thought, which meant there was a good chance of John still being alive. Mill sent her love and hoped he was all right and that he would be home soon.

'Home soon' and 'hope you are all right' if only she knew. Then he thought it was probably better that she didn't know. He wondered if any of them back home had any idea what it was like to be stuck out there in this God forsaken trench, being bombed, shot at and seeing your mates dying or blown to pieces in front of you. Already he was having nightmares where he saw men sliding into the mud to a slow suffocating death.

A sudden burst from a rifle and the shout of, "Got you, you bastard!" caused Jesse to turn around. One of his fellow comrades had got a German who was running near the occupied trenches on the other side of 'no-man's land'. This strip of land, no more than a hundred yards wide at this point was all that separated the Germans from the British Tommie's.

The rest of the day and following night passed fairly quietly with little enemy activity, but with daybreak the noise of a hostile aeroplane could be heard approaching. As it came into sight the gunners in the trench opened fire with their A.A. guns and the plane retreated, but it came back again the following morning. This time it received a hit and as it slowly descended back over the enemy line the men gave a loud cheer.

A few days later after heavy shelling during the night from both sides, a voice was heard calling out from the German Trenches and in perfect English, "Gentleman of the Queen's, how are you today?"

A few choice words were called back in return.

Jesse sat on the step of the trench and shook his head in disbelief. Here they were all trying to kill each other, not because they wanted to, but because they had to if they wanted to survive themselves. The rats were running along the trenches and the lice were driving them mad and some one calls out 'How are you?' as if they were passing on opposite sides of the street back home. Jesse wondered why they didn't all call it a day, pack up their gear and all sod off. Trouble was, neither side had the choice; they had to go on with it whether they wanted to or not or be shot for desertion, either way they didn't have much chance.

Suddenly a bright spark near to Jesse stood up on the trench step and shouted at the top of his voice,

"I'm fed up with this bloody war, I wanna go 'ome and go up the pub!"

"For Christ sake get yer bleeding 'ead down!" Jesse yelled at him, "they'll bloody well 'ave you!

A German shouted a reply in his own language, which they couldn't understand.

"If you've got something to say", yelled a young Private, "then say it in English! Bloody foreigners" he mumbled.

"If it's your round then we will have 500 pints of your very best bitter please gentleman of the Queen's!" came the instant reply in English.

Someone shouted back, "Piss off!" and that brought the conversation to a close.

Jesse wondered what would happen if they walked across with a crate of Ben Truman's? Would the Germans be grateful and shake their hands and give them a chance to get back to the trenches before opening fire? Most likely they would which just went to show the whole dam stupidity of this stinking bloody war.

Not long after this, Jesse was astonished to hear that they were going to be relieved by the 9th. Devonshire's; John Samuels regiment!

On the morning the relief battalion arrived Jesse eagerly looked amongst the men for his old mate from back home. There would be about half an hour to spare before their Commanders exchanged notes and information and the march back to Bray.

Jesse went over to the new arrivals and asked several groups if they knew where he might find anyone by the name of Samuels. He had been a Private when Jesse last saw him, but of course could have been promoted by now. Several men were unloading their backpacks and Jesse walked over to where they were and asked again,

"Anyone know if there's a John Samuels around?" he asked.

"Yeah, who wants to know?" a soldier with his back to Jesse asked.

Jesse couldn't believe his ears and as the man turned round both were dumbstruck.

"Bloody Hell! Is that you Jesse?"

Jesse had grown a moustache since being out there, but John recognised him immediately

Suddenly the two mates were throwing their arms around each other almost crying and unable to believe that they had met up so far from home and Bethnal Green. They were delighted to know both were still amongst the living and had survived against the most tremendous odds.

They talked until it was time for Jesse to leave and John had to take up his position in the trenches. They hoped they would meet up again somewhere soon and maybe have a drink if they ever got the chance. They knew that was wishful thinking but as the two mates parted they were both smiling and felt happiness that had long since been forgotten.

One month led into another then towards the end of June 1916 word went around that the 'Big Push' which had been talked about since way back when Jesse had first joined up was finally going to take place.

'How long ago was that?' he asked himself and was amazed when he realised it was seventeen months. It could have easily been seventeen years; it certainly felt more like years than months.

"We've heard it all before", Jesse said to the Private who had told him the news.

"No, its true this time, they reckon it will be on the 1st July".

"Well, I'll believe it when I see it" Jesse said as he smashed a spade down onto the head of a rat that was just about to investigate the contents of his backpack.

News also came that Lord Kitchener who had encouraged them to join up with his posters declaring that their country needed them to fight was dead. He'd been on his way to Russia on a special government mission when his ship had been sunk by the German Navy. Jesse didn't feel any compassion; he just thought that the bloke who had encouraged so many thousands to sign on was now just another name on the list of those missing or dead. Kitchener must have been lucky; drowning was a much better and quicker way to go than die in a slow agonising way or being blown to kingdom come.

However within a few days it was obvious that this Big Push was eventually going to take place and the young Private had got the information correct. Hundreds upon hundreds of new recruits were being drafted in daily and conscription was now compulsory by law. Ammunition was arriving almost hourly by the truckload.

Sometimes when there was a brief chance to lay his head against the wall of the trench for a few minutes rest Jesse thought of the men who had been miners before the war now digging tunnels under the ground edging their way quietly and slowly forwards towards the German lines. The heads of these tunnels were to be packed with explosives that would be set off before the big advance on the morning of the 1st July

Jesse felt real sorry for these blokes who were working under ground. He had heard of a team of miners who had gone in to change shifts and by the light of lanterns found a man almost dead just a few yards in. He had a bad wound to his head and had obviously tried to crawl back to the entrance. Someone went for stretcher-bearers while the others went on.

It seems that there were no lights at the end of the tunnel, which was unusual and when the men got there they found all their fellow men dead. At first they thought there had been an accident and the roof had caved in leaving several half buried. But then they noticed some had gunshot wounds and lying among them was a German with a spade imbedded in his chest. It was obvious that they had unfortunately broken into a trench being dug by the enemy coming towards them.

Bravely they had all fought for their lives but died where the two tunnels had met and then caved in blocking the German side. No doubt many other miners from both sides now lay dead beneath the rubble. Jesse thought it was bad enough fighting above on the ground, but underneath in a tunnel must have been a hundred times worse.

At the time the preparations were taking place for this big push Jesse's Battalion was at Bois Des Taillies and it was here that the men were briefed as to the situation and given details of the forthcoming plans.

There were six days left until the end of June and that time was to be spent knocking the hell out of the Germans. Their trenches were to be bombed and shelled continuously day and night until it was almost impossible for any of them to have survived. Then at 7.30 a.m. on the first day of July one and a half million British and Allied soldiers, spread along fifteen miles of trenches would go forward, one line behind the other to flush out any of the enemy who were still alive.

And so the bombardment began, hour after hour bombs and shells exploded over enemy lines. The trucks kept doing return trips to keep the supplies of ammunition stacked up and the noise was the worst the men had ever heard. There was no letting up, hour after hour for six days and six nights and then finally it stopped and all was quiet. There had been some retaliation from the German side during the first couple of days but they were soon in a state of silence. After the battering they had taken it would be a miracle if any of them had escaped with their lives. The war was about to end and the clearing up was about to begin.

At 1.30 a.m. Jesse and his whole Battalion having marched from Bois Des Tailles assembled at a place called Grantown in the Somme Valley. Here they rested for 30 minutes and were given water and two bandoleers (shoulder belts with loops for cartridges) after which the Battalion proceeded by Companies to their positions in the support trenches. A few hours later two of the tunnels packed with explosives under the enemy lines were detonated and the biggest bang ever heard in history went off. The ground shook as if an earthquake had struck and it was later reported that the sound of the explosion was heard back in England. The men had been prepared for it, but nothing could have warned them of the deafening noise and for many their hearing would be permanently impaired if not lost completely forever.

Once in position a few rounds were fired from the front line to see the strength of any remaining enemy. Surprisingly there had been more gunfire returned than had been anticipated, especially after the six days of heavy shelling and that morning's almighty explosions. Earth had even rained down covering many of the soldiers waiting to advance in the trenches and others had to dig trenches clear to release their own men.

Those in Command were convinced that the amount of cross fire was nothing the men couldn't handle and expected it to be the final battle of the War.

As dawn broke, it was obvious that it was going to be a lovely day at least weather wise. Already it was getting warm and as the sun came up a beautiful morning was born giving promise for a perfect day with a cloudless sky and temperatures reaching 72 degrees.

At 7.30 a.m. the whistles were blown and one and a half million men moved forward and so began the bloodiest day in the history of World War One. This was the start of the Battle of the Somme.

Chapter Six

The Battle of the Somme July 1916. 7th. Division
Part One

"Nearly time Jesse" a young fresh faced lad said as he fumbled to fix a bayonet to a Lee Enfield rifle that was nearly as big as its owner.

"Yeah" was the short reply. Jesse Warren was not in a talking mood today. His throat was dry and he wondered how the hell this young kid who hadn't even started shaving yet had passed as being old enough to join the bloody army in the first place. Then he remembered the day he had joined up himself and how the Recruiting Sergeant had encouraged another young lad to lie about his age.

'Sixteen!' Jesse shook his head in disbelief as he looked at the lad who was slightly taller than himself and no more than a kid.

He'd only been with the regiment a few days and somehow had attached himself to Jesse. He'd told him his name was Frank and he'd lied about his age, in fact he had only turned sixteen a few months back. This would be his first time in serious action

A Sergeant standing nearby was talking to the lad,

"Give it here son" he said as he easily snapped the bayonet into position and as he did so, pulled the lads tin hat down over his eyes with a chuckle. Jesse smiled.

All along the trench they were peering over the parapet and Jesse was no exception. Ahead he could see the crouched figures of the 22nd Manchester's and could just make out their Northern drawl. To the left were the 1st. South Staffordshire's with the kilted figures of the 2nd Gordon Highlander's further on. Further on still he could just make out the distant figures of the 9th Devonshire's.

'Good luck John', Jesse said softly under his breath for he knew that one of those distant bodies was that of his old mate and neighbour from back home, John Samuels. His thoughts went to Mill and John's wife Hetty. Hopefully it would be all over soon and they would both be going home.

A sudden rush of air bought Jesse back to reality and he fell backwards into the safety of the trench. A dull 'crump' told him that a shell had gone over and the cries and calls for the medics soon told him it had hit the 21st Manchester's who were in the trench behind.

"Gangway! Gangway!" yelled a cockney voice to the right.

A huge Lance Corporal appeared half-running, half falling. A khaki coloured sack was over his shoulder and as he passed blood could be seen dripping from the sack.

"Blimey!" gasped the young lad," there's a man in there".

The Sergeant standing nearby told them it was one of the Royal Fusiliers who had copped it. As the body passes by, another young chap to the left of Jesse collapsed.

"Hey you there!" shouts the Lieutenant to a soldier standing next to the slumped man, "Help him up!"

It was Private Hughs who tried to assist the man and as he nudged his arm he took two steps back in terror. Nobody had heard George Summers die.

"Cover him up", said the Sergeant.

Already the day was getting warmer. A call was passed along the lines,

"Ready?.....ready!"

Hastily whispered prayers and low mumbles suddenly rose from the trenches and those of Catholic domination made the sign of the cross.

The only thing that came to Jesse's mind was,

"Oh, shit! Here we go again".

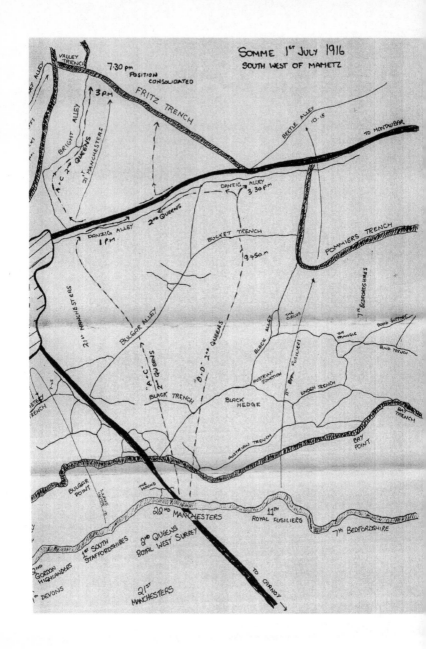

SOMME 1st JULY 1916
SOUTH WEST OF MAMETZ

For a few seconds it was deadly quiet, a complete silence. One and a half million men and boys stood together with their hearts pounding. Then the whistles could be heard all along the lines, "Go!" yells the Lieutenant and quickly disappears over the top. Jesse followed. The young boy follows and so do the others. There didn't appear to be a rush, some of the Queen's East Surrey's further down the line had taken several footballs with them and were kicking the balls to each other as they crossed no man's land. Jesse makes it to the next trench just vacated by the 22nd Manchester's ahead.

Suddenly he sees the Manchester's charge and just as suddenly he sees them die. A man to the right is caught in the barbed wire, another flies vertically upright and another simply disappears. They press on, crossing the 'Mound' and Bulger Trench with very little resistance. They advance further and suddenly a few German soldiers appear behind the Manchester's and shoot at the Tommie's backs. Rapid fire from the Queen's soon silence them.

Jesse wondered if he'd got the one without the jacket or had someone else. Either way, they had got most of them.

A group of the Boch has had enough and trots towards the Queen's; these were taken prisoner and headed back to base. Several others appeared from hiding and aimed towards them, none made it.

"I didn't come 'ere to take that lot 'ome with me" grunts the Sarge as he lowers his gun. Life was very cheap that day.

Machine guns hosed at the Manchester's as they stormed on. The German gunners dug in at Danzig Alley and nearby Mametz think the advancing Tommie's must be crazy. Jesse thinks they must be crazy too, where the hell were all these Jerries coming from? They were led to believe that they had been annihilated over the past week but here they were coming out of nowhere, like the rats in the trenches.

Crazy they may be, but so far they have covered 700 yards. Jesse had run as fast as he could until his heart was pounding and he gasped for breath. The weight of his backpack and the full bandoleers didn't help either. He was well pissed off by now and realised that it wasn't going to be the cushy walkover they had all been led to believe. Once again in this God forsaken war, Jesse was in the thick of it and he knew his chances of survival were pretty grim.

The Stafford's take Cemetery Trench and a few cheers go up the Lieutenant along side Jesse shouts,

"Good show lads!" as some of the Manchester's make it on to Bucket trench.

Jesse follows and is suddenly thrown to the ground as shellfire surrounds them. Several are killed and a man near to Jesse has half his leg blown away and is screaming in agony just a few yards in front is the trench.

"Help me pull him into the trench", Jesse shouts to Frank who has stuck by his side since the whistles went.

Together they crawl across the rough ground pulling the screaming man until they reach back to the trench and fall in. They all have a soft landing and Jesse turns to see several dead men sprawled across each other. Staring unseeing eyes look into Jesse's, but he's seen it all before and isn't repulsed.

Several other 'Queen's' fall into the trench too, but these are the unlucky ones, their bodies fall as severed limbs splatter against the walls.

Jesse and the young boy, who stuck to him like glue, moved along in the trench stepping over bodies and find a space where several men were crouching. Some are from the Queen's.

They wait there catching their breath and the lieutenant, who was with Jesse's group passed his field glasses and said,

"Take a look over and see what you make of it," gesturing at an enemy position to the right.

Jesse focused on the distant excitement and stared in astonishment as flashes from guns and bayonets glinted in the strong sunlight. Vicious hand to hand fighting was taking place. Jesse had never fought hand to hand with the Germans; his fighting had always been from behind a rifle. The thoughts of having to go in like the poor bastards already out in front turned his stomach over. Although they'd had bayonet practise when in training Jesse didn't know if he could actually thrust the deadly blade into another man's body. He knew if he was confronted with the situation there wouldn't be any choice; it would either be the German or himself.

Before he could dwell further on these thoughts, a strange 'plopping' noise filled his ears and as he turned he saw the lieutenant standing upright with a bullet hole right through the middle of his eyes. A Sergeant knocked the man to the ground, as the young lad was sick.

By this time the South Staffordshire's had reached the ruins of Mametz, but the Fritz were not pleased and put up some resistance. The Staffordshire's fell back to Cemetery trench, but for many their day was done; their life was done.

A red flare arcs over the now scarred and burned countryside. It was only just after 9.30a.m and it had taken two hours to get this far .A call went out,

"2nd Queen's! Let's go!" Jesse starts running, this time he was running for his life. The lad was still keeping close, as was the Sergeant and several others.

The noise was terrific as mud and steel fragments were flying in all directions. Jesse jumped down into Bulger trench and once again had a soft landing. He landed on the torn body of a young Manchester who could have only been about nineteen years old.

'Poor sod', Jesse thought as he gasped for breath.

"Keep going! Keep going!" yelled a voice from somewhere, "Up! Up! Up!"

Jesse climbed up and over the top and ran. The noise was deafening and the smoke obstructed his view. He looked round for the lad, he was still with him,

"Come on son! come on! Keep with me, keep going, for God's sake keep going!" Jesse didn't even know where *he* was going, but they kept running.

An arm detached from it's body flew past in front of Jesse's path and as he ran around a shell hole filled with mud he noticed a pair of legs waving wildly in the air. There was no time to help anyone now he just had to keep running.

Jesse thought he must be in front of the others; there was hardly anyone with him. Maybe he was in front, maybe he wasn't, he just didn't know, but there weren't many runners in the race now.

He could hear a different sound amongst the tremendous din, which reminded him of a locomotive letting off steam at Bethnal Green station.

'Bethnal Green?' he thought, 'where the hell is that?' Was it some place he once knew before he had been dragged out here?

"Christ knows!" he thought and realised the continuous hissing sound he could hear was German Maxim machine gun fire and crouched down low while he still kept running. Never in his life had he ran so hard. Bodies were everywhere and he tried not to fall over them. His lungs were almost bursting and just on the point of collapse when he saw a trench in front of him.

He wondered whether it was Black trench or was it Red trench? Or was that behind him? The whole world seemed to have gone mad. One of the Manchester's was wandering around asking the time. Jesse pushed him out of the way as he made his final spurt and then heard the familiar drawl of the Manchester's urging him and the lad on into Bucket trench. They fell in and landed in a puddle of crimson mud.

Jesse wished he could take his backpack off as he gasped for breath. He thought he was going to die. Excruciating pain was spreading across his chest as his lungs and heart was stretched beyond their endurance. The pounding of his heart matched the thumping in his head and he closed his eyes over a painful red haze. The sweat was pouring from him and he tried to loosen the collar of his tunic. His throat was parched and he felt his end was near. Maybe death would be a happy release from this hell. Through the red haze he could see the young lad on his knees struggling for breath and there was nothing he could do to help him.

'Perhaps we'll go together', Jesse thought, 'after all, the lad's stuck by me all this time,'

Gradually the pain began to ease and breathing came easier. He was still alive. Someone gave him a sip of water from his canteen.

"Thanks mate,"

When he was able he asked one of the Manchester's where the rest of their men where.

"Behind you mate" came the reply, "you've just run over them. There ain't any more left."

Jesse looked around, the lad was still alive and so was the Sergeant who had been with them, along with a surprising number of the 'Queen's'.

Jesse listened, between the bullets firing overhead and the whizz-bangs he could hear German voices shouting to each other. The Boche were that close! They were in Danzig Alley, the next trench.

Then the shout came from the Sergeant,

"Queen's…. Move!".

"Oh, Christ no!", but Jesse was up and running again. Anger got to all of them as the Queen's ran forward screaming like wild demons as they charged Dazig Alley straight into a rain of hot lethal lead. Men were falling, their time had come. In front of them a huge barrage erupts as their own big guns from behind hit their target.

"Thank Christ for that!" some one near by shouted.

The Huns were off guard and yielded to the bayonets of the 'English devils',

"Kammerad!, kammearad!. Ich libe mine kinde….bitter" whimpers a huge Prussian before a bayonet pierces his throat.

"What's he say?" asked a voice from behind.

'Blimey!' Jesse thought, 'it's the lad!'

"Christ! you're still with us son!"

As a soldier retrieved his bloody bayonet he told them that he thought the Prussian had said something about kids and surrendering.

By now the Queen's had won the eastern part of Danzig Alley and special bombers from their regiment crept westward to flush out any remaining resistance. This time Jesse had to crawl northwards up to Bright Alley, which was the next trench in front. This was particularly terrifying. At least when running there is no time to think but crawling on ones stomach was like doing things in slow motion. The enemy started lobbing grenades and then charged firing a few rounds at the leading men and then ran back.

Those of the Queen's, who had made it so far, reached Bright Alley where men from various other regiments were already there. Jesse pressed himself against the wall of the trench as specialist flame throwing teams called,

"Make way! Make way!" as they passed along the trench with their equipment.

Seconds later the most hideous screams met the ears of the men and worst still was the smell of burning flesh. The screaming went on and on until some of the Queens broke cover and fired at the running masses of flames. They could not take the screams.

Having taken Bright Alley they went on to take Fritz trench and there at last they had a chance to rest. By now it was 6.30 p.m. and they had not slept since the day before. For eleven hours they had carried their rifles, ran towards the enemy and staring death in the face, defied it.

Exhausted and utterly spent, Jesse sat on the firing step in the trench with his back against the wall and pondered over the last eleven hours. Was it eleven hours he asked himself or was it eleven minutes? Time didn't have meaning any more.

He remembered seeing a lance corporal with no jaw who had once played a mouth organ. The German in his underwear wearing a spiked helmet who was running around in the midst of it all with a kettle. The mutilated horses, men entangled in barbed wire bleeding profusely in a slow death. Fields that had once been green were now nothing but churned up earth covered with blood and the bodies of those whose lives had been taken away. Burnt and charred smouldering remains that just a short time ago had been gallant men, regardless to the fact that they were German remains, now lay with blackened faces showing their last agonising moments.

Jesse let out a big sigh, he had made it through and so had the lad,

"You alright son?"

"Yeah, I think so" he replied. Jesse got his backpack off and retrieved his own water canteen and the boy did likewise. Jesse vowed that if he were lucky enough to get through this lot he would always remember that drink of water. Although it was warm from the heat of the sun, to him it was better than a pint of Ben Truman's had ever been.

Jesse noticed the boy was shaking; in fact they were all shaking. Some of the men could take no more and had their heads in their hands sobbing. A man took his rifle and held it to his head, the sound echoed along the trench.

Another began praying quietly,

"Our Father, who art in heaven".... other's joined in with soft mumbles,

"Hallowed be thy name, thy Kingdom come...."

There were still some of the Queens in the trench and men from various other regiments. Many of them had no idea whether they had been coming or going during the smoke and hours of intense firing and shelling. Some were still disoriented and had no idea which way was forward or which way was backwards.

Several South Stafford's were in the trench along with a group of Manchester's and even some 'kilties'.

Jesse thought of back home and knew that his chances of ever returning were very slight. He still had Bert's pencil in his breast pocket and finding a discarded cigarette packet, wrote a note to Mill.

He had done his best and no one could expect more. He put the note in his pocket and then remembered John Samuels. Jesse had no way of knowing that the 9th. Devon's had been slaughtered by machine gun fire from Fricourt Wood and many a Tommy had died before reaching Mansel Copse. The chance of ever seeing his old mate again was now very remote indeed.

Somehow rations had reached through and Jesse realised he was starving and hadn't eaten since late the night before,

'When was that?' he asked himself thinking that last night could have been years ago. It certainly seemed so now he'd had a chance to rest. Orders were given to 'dig in' for the night.

"Christ! " Jesse yelled out as a magazine of the Kaisers finest lead zips into the sandbag he was just about to throw onto the parapet, "that was bloody close!".

It was even closer for their Lt. Col. Alandice who had just walked past Jesse and for Private Mortimer who were both tall men. Men of their height suffered in the trenches and Jesse was grateful that he was only a short man and could keep his head down.

A second Lieutenant yells out that every forth man is on lookout.

Jesse swore under his breath when he found he was a 'fourth man' and gingerly raised his head into the view of the eagle-eyed snipers spread along the German line. Like giant raindrops in a muddy puddle, splashes of light could be seen along the front. Trees were being ripped to shreds and the landscape had changed beyond all recognition. A shell exploded close to where Jesse was standing on the firing step and he pressed his face into the dirt.

A soldier fell into the trench behind Jesse and he spun around in surprise but lowered his rifle when he saw that it was one of his own men who had somehow managed to crawl across the field minus his right leg. Others tried to make the chap as comfortable as they could, but how can you be comfortable with a leg blown away?

Jesse thought it strange that the man wasn't feeling any pain and thought it must be the shock that had numbed him.

A few more gasping men had fallen into the trench at intervals and some were lucky to have missed being hit by gunfire. Two others were blown in and dead before they hit the ground, a couple of chaps didn't seem to know where they were since being separated from their regiments.

Jesse turned to look, "You're still on lookout Warren!" a Sergeant brawled, "Get back to your post!"

Jesse mumbled a few oaths and did as he was bid.

"Something's happening!" called another 'fourth man' and some of the men sneaked a look over the top while trying to keep their heads low in case of snipers.

He got back on the step and in the distance could see clouds of what looked like smoke, then he realised,

"They're letting off the gas!" he cried out

"Christ!" someone said, "what'll we do? We ain't got any gas masks!"

"Just pee in your handkerchiefs and wrap 'em round your faces!" another voice replied, "It's the only chance you've got!"

"Keep your head down" Jesse warned the bloke next to him, but it was too late.

Suddenly there was an almighty noise as a shell whizzed over the trench and as he ducked Jesse heard the most indescribable sound that would stay with him for the rest of his life. The young solider who'd been firing next to him had been hit and his head was completely blown away.

Jesse was absolutely stunned. He stood there covered in splattered blood and saw the headless body lying in the trench as blood pumped from a gapping neck. It bubbled and made a gurgling noise as if protesting from deep within. In a state of shock Jesse looked for his head but it had gone. Pieces of flesh and blood running down the wall of the trench behind him were all that remained. Jesse suddenly threw up, but all he could do was painfully retch on an empty stomach.

Anger and hate swept through him as he let out a terrifying roar in anguish and began screaming a torrent of abuse at the Germans who had just blown the head from a fellow country man, just some ordinary bloke like himself. He hastily reloaded his rifle and went to go over the top swearing and cursing in desperation,

"I'll kill the fucking lot of 'em!" he screamed, "I'll kill every last one of the bleeders!"

Someone had grabbed him and was pulling him back. He just didn't have the strength to resist and fell back into the trench where he sat and sobbed like a baby. He began shaking uncontrollably and felt a cigarette being put in his mouth.

"Come on mate," someone said sympathetically, "He's gone now."

The young solider had been covered with some old sacking, but Jesse could not help seeing the huge pool of dark blood seeping into the soil.

An arm went around his shoulder, it was Frank,

"Come on mate, he's out of this stinking war now, at least he got it quick not like some of the poor buggers screaming in agony until they're dead.

Jesse took comfort from the words of a man, who just a few months ago had been a sixteen year old kid, probably playing 'Knock Down Ginger' or football with his mates in a back street somewhere.

The only way Jesse could deal with this horrific butchery was to keep telling himself that it had been 'just another man' among the many thousands who had gone down. Hadn't he seen men die in the most gruesome and horrifying way almost every day he'd been out there?

He told himself that it was just another unfortunate bloke but inside his heart was crying at the utter stupidity of a bitter, senseless war.

A slight breeze had come up and changed the direction of the distant gas. Jesse hoped it would turn towards the Germans and let them get a taste of their own medicine and suffer a slow agonising and lingering painful death, choking on the acid fumes with their lungs burning like fire.

During the early hours of the following morning he did another lookout shift but he was finding it very difficult to keep his eyes open. He once heard of two blokes getting shot for falling asleep on duty and he hadn't come this far to be shot for the same thing. He was thankful when Billy King a chap he had got to know from Lewisham, came along to relieve him.

While the remaining British and their Allies slept, the Germans were preparing their machine gun posts ready for a second massacre.

For those on lookout it was hard to tell the sleeping men from the dead but it made no difference to the rats. Like the Germans, they came out from their holes deep in the ground having survived every thing that they had been thrown at them during the long hot day. The only difference was that the Germans were attacking their enemy, the rats weren't fussy.

Chapter Seven

The Battle of the Somme: 2nd. July
Part Two

With the dawning of the second day Jesse could see the fields of German dead before him. Word had gone along the line to prepare for action and nervous fingers collected the necessary kit. Jesse could sense eyes staring at him, eager for blood.

At 7.30 a.m. The whistles blew,

"It's bleeding 7.30 again!" Jesse shouts to no-one in particular.

A Corporal he knew as Shaw called back,

"Yeah, we might as well 'ave posted the bloody Kaiser a letter to say we're coming!"

Jesse climbed over the top and as he did so Corporal Lionel Shaw who was just along to the left was thrown back into the trench.

Jesse knew he had to keep going but it was difficult over dead bodies and churned up ground. He fell and as he did dropped his rifle but was soon up and running again. As well as collecting his rifle he collected his wits and realised to his amazement that he was still alive but knew he had to run.

He heard a voice shouting, "Keep going, keep going!" and then realised it was his own. He looked around for the young lad who had been beside him all of yesterday, but he couldn't see him. He kept running as mud and gravel showered down on the sprinting men.

They were on top of the enemy position by now and a Second Lieutenant named Geary waved the men on. Jesse followed firing all the time. Bayonets were slicing into German flesh and bullets were missing him by inches.

For the defenders it was now too much and they had a real fear of British steel. A tubby German fell to his knees in front of Jesse and began throwing wild empty hands up towards the sky. He stopped in front of him and held his bayonet to the man's throat who was now screaming in terror but he didn't push it in, he didn't know if he could really do it, he just stood there looking into clear blue German eyes. Suddenly it wasn't his problem any more. One of the Queen's, Albert Bower dragged the German away and shoved him along with the other 24 men who had been taken prisoners.

Jesse was soaked in sweat and could feel the lice under his armpits and on his body. The tin helmet was burning into his head under the heat of the sun,

"God almighty!" he cried out, looking at the death and destruction all around him, "What the fucking 'ell 'ave we done to deserve this?"

The heat was stifling and it wasn't yet mid-day. Bluebottles were buzzing around and homing in on the dead and exposed flesh. Some tried to land on Jesse's arm and he brushed them away with his free hand,

"Piss off you bastards!" he shouted, "I ain't bleeding dead yet!"

White trench and Queens Nullah had now been taken and a Second Lieutenant named Jacobs had hold of a German machine gun which he swung round and faced it towards its former owners.

Looking eastward Jesse saw that the 8th. Devon's had taken Orchard trench North and a cheer went up amongst the men.

One of the Queen's, Private Passmore called along the line,

"News is we're to stay put for now!"

"Thank Christ for that!" Jesse said as they all sighed with relief. The rest of the day was spent consolidating the position with wiring parties and stretcher-bearers running to and fro. Further down the line the trench had fallen in from the force of yet another explosion and frantic fingers dug out the entombed men. Seeing the sudden activity, snipers from the other side started taking pot shots at the bobbing heads. Then the bobbing heads started firing back. Everyone seemed O.K. apart from cuts and bruising.   One of the men was suddenly blown out of the trench, but only smouldering khaki came down to earth, another soldier 'Known only to God'

Someone calls out, "How many more do you want Mr. Haig!" The British High Commander cannot hear him, he's is safely tucked away out of danger.

A terrific barrage then ripped through Mametz Woods in front of the Queen's, sending trees, plants and nature into oblivion. Two tunnels packed with 24 tons of explosives had been detonated but the Germans had dug down deep in their concrete shelters and only got shaken up. Jesse was glad it was his own side's shells whistling overhead and not from the Berlin built guns.

The British guns had been made by the women back home and they worked day and night to keep the men in ammunition. Jesse thought of all the sweethearts, aunts, sisters, mothers, wives and widows that kept them going. Thousands didn't even know they were widowed yet and as many mothers didn't know their sons were lying dead in this God forsaken land. He had lost count of the many times he had taken Mill's picture from inside his tunic pocket.

She'd had it taken just after they'd married and he made sure he had it with him before he left home. 'When was that?' he wondered...'a million years ago?' The photo was now dirty and tatty but just looking down at her lovely face gave him the will to live.

Some blokes who just couldn't take any more had held their riffles to their heads and fired. He had to keep his sanity; he had Mill and the girls waiting for him at home, "Oh God", he cried "Please God, help me!"

Night began to fall again and just as he was dozing off, Jesse felt a tug on his arm and jumped.

It was Frank.

"You dozy bugger!" Jesse shouted at him, "I nearly bloody well shot yer!"

But he was pleased to see the boy had got through and asked where he had been.

"I dunno," he replied, "I just sort of followed on, but I got some Jesse! I got some!" and then he began to cry.

"Come on son, you'll be all right", Jesse put a comforting arm around the lads shoulders, "you'll be all right". It was now his turn to comfort the boy.

All the men had truly been through the gates of hell and were sitting waiting for them to open again. Jesse knew this lad had seen more in the last 48 hours than anyone back home could possibly ever imagine. He came out to France a young lad of sixteen and it took just a few hours to turn him into a man.

"St. Peter will be busy tonight," he was saying,

"Yeah" Jesse replied, "let's hope he's got plenty of room".

All too soon the night passed uneasily and thunderstorms and lightning could be seen towards the Southeast. The gentle rumbling was music after the ear-splitting crashes of the guns.

Stalemate seemed to have settled along the trench and for the next twelve days the men of the Queen's were on constant alert for snipers and the first sign of enemy barrage.

Jesse looked along the trench at the scene, bodies were slowly being cleared, but the stench lingered. More and more rats were appearing, Jesse wondered where they all kept coming from, it was as if they were sending messages to other rats to come and see what they were missing. The nights were the worst; they would start gnawing at a man while he was sleeping. It didn't matter to the rats whether they were dead or alive, but a swift kick or the butt of a rifle soon told them otherwise.

It was now the 14th July and Jesse suddenly remembered it was Mill's birthday.

He wondered what she was doing and thoughts of home started to fill his mind. He remembered the day he'd walked out of Gratton Houses to join up. He remembered the coal man who said he would join up and take his 'Bloody 'orses' with him. A lump came into his throat and he felt tears on his mud-splattered face. He tried to put thoughts of home behind him; it was too painful to think of what he may never see again. He had Mill's photograph in his tunic pocket and it gave him comfort to know that she would be with him if his luck didn't hold out and the next bullet or shell had his name on it. The following day they were all informed that they were to charge High Wood just south east of the town of Martinguich. "Sod that" Jesse remarked to a group of men cramped around an early brew of what should have been tea, but certainly didn't taste like it. "Yeah", someone replied, "don't fancy our chances at that!" And so on the 15th July at 9a.m., it all began again.

What was left of the 2nd Queen's, the 1st. South Staffordshire's and the 21st Manchester's went over the top together. Jesse, like all the other's felt they could not take much more as they started running again. On and forward they went, men were falling like autumn leaves. The Boche knew they were coming and were ready for them.

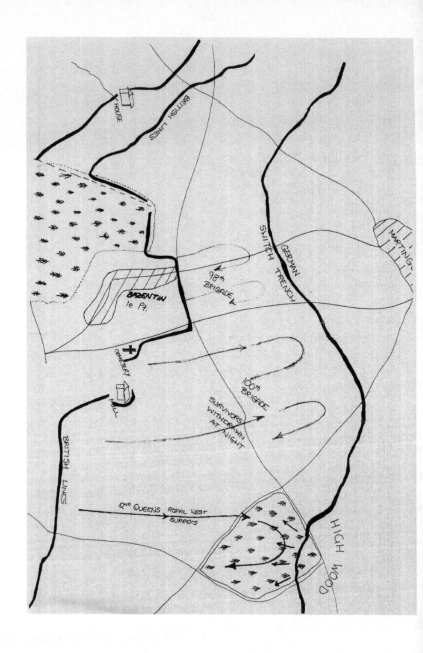

Jesse made it to the woods and fell hard against a fallen log. He looked around and could only see about half of his mates still alive. A few very brave Tommies tried to press forward to the trench known as Switch trench where the Germans were strongly placed but were easily cut down.

Unbelievably, orders were given again to charge and Jesse found himself deeper in the cool woods with twigs, mud and leaves flying in all directions. Men fell at every yard until the Queens could go no further. Jesse hid the best he could, he dare hardly breathe. He knew some others were about but he kept very still and quiet. Suddenly the sixteen year old lad came crashing through the under growth and threw himself down beside the terrified Jesse.

"For Christ sake keep quiet!" Jesse hissed at him and the boy did as he was bid. For the next five and half-hours they both kept very still and very quiet indeed.

By half past two they could make out the massed lines of the 1st. Queen's and the 9th highland light infantry charging the open ground to the east,

"It's bloody suicide," whispered Jesse in horror and disgust, "They haven't got a chance in hell".

The neat lines of men were being torn to ribbons and those still standing started running back towards where Jesse and the lad were in hiding. The retreating men were being fired upon all the way and fell like ninepins. It was utter carnage as bodies were thrown up in the air and landed on those already dead.

Suddenly a great roar went up as hundred's of German voices screamed and rushed towards them.

The remaining Queens fled as fast as they could towards the woods and only a few survivors were left by the time they reached there.

Jesse and the lad had got up and ran straight into two Highland Light Infantry Officer's who yelled at them,

"Hold your ground! Get back and hold your ground!" and threatened to shoot if they did not obey the order.

"Sod off Jock!" someone called and they all continued running, shots were being fired.

The lad looked behind him and screamed in terror, "Look at that bloody lot, we've had it now!"

Hundreds of Germans were nearing the woods and they felt the bullets whiz past from their guns and heard the cries of those who had been hit. They kept going and when they found themselves in a thicker part of the High Wood they hid in a concealed shell hole. It was their only chance.

How they survived that dreadful charge they never knew. They stayed in the shell hole for two days hardly talking, hardly moving and just living on the last drops of water in their canteens. It was so hot during the day, but the shade of the trees gave them a cool cover. During the first night rustling leaves filled them with dread and they waited for a German revolver to appear over the top of the shell hole. But they need not have worried; it was just the rats that almost out numbered the Germans. They didn't bother with Jesse or the lad, there were enough already dead for them to bother with the living. The Germans had made it easy for the rodents.

They hadn't had their boots or clothes off for days and the lice were breading like wildfire. Jesse felt he couldn't go on any more and if it hadn't been for the young sixteen-year-old he might have just closed his eyes and given up. Occasionally they heard a few shots as the Germans search parties found other hiding soldiers. They certainly weren't taking any of them prisoners. Every time Jesse heard a gun fired, he knew another poor sod had got it.

After the second day, things were very quiet until that evening when the Royal Artillery began shelling the wood in retaliation. They couldn't stand being in that hole any more, especially with the chance of being killed by their own men. Once again they began running and as the shock waves from the increasing shells became too much to bare they threw themselves into the nearest shell hole for refuge. Five others were all ready occupying the hole but they would not make any comment on the sudden intrusion. Their lives had ended several days before and all that remained now was the raw rotting flesh and blood soaked remnants of uniforms. The smell was sickening and the noise was deafening. Jesse didn't know what the worst of the two was and put his trembling hands over his ears and tightly closed his eyes. He marvelled at the way he and the lad had kept together throughout this long ordeal let alone the fact that they were both still alive while thousands lay around them dead.

The firing kept up and they were continually showered with chalky soil but were spared any serious injury.

Meanwhile the remainder of the 2nd Queen's and the rest of the 91st Brigade had made it back to the British lines and by the following morning of Sunday the 16th were gathered in shell holes at the relatively safe area of Bazentine-le-Grand.

The roll calls were performed which didn't take long. There weren't many that had survived.

As the shelling decreased around them, Jesse and his young companion climbed out from their place of refuge and began crawling on their bellies back towards the British lines and nervously waited for a sniper's bullet. This could quite easily come from an eager Fritz crack shot or a terrified Tommie who would shoot first and ask questions after but so far so good, all was quiet.

On they went into another shell hole where they found several dead Queens', but it was the only chance of cover while they caught their breath and had a short rest.

The weary pair decided to wait until dark before making the last final dash back.

"What about those Jock Officers Jesse, do you think they would have fired at us?"

"I think they did mate but we went through so fast, I didn't have time to look!"

The lad was worried, "But supposing they got through and recognise us when we get back and 'ave us for doing a runner? Surely they won't think we were cowards, will they Jesse?"

"Cowards! How the bloody hell could anyone call us cowards after what we've been through since we've been out here in this bloody God forsaken dump? We wouldn't 'ave 'ad a chance when that lot came charging towards us, it would have been suicide, we might as well have pinned a note on our tunics saying, 'Shoot me," then he mumbled to himself, "and they will probably say we we're cowards...sod the bloody lot of 'em

He felt he had reached the end of his endurance many times and still wondered how he had kept his sanity. And as for a lad having to suffer the horror of seeing men torn apart and risking his own life …well he deserved a medal, but all Jesse said with a grumble was,

"Well let's hope we don't meet up with those two then."

He knew thousands had died and felt utter repulsion, young men had bravely gone forward following orders knowing they were going to their deaths, they had no chance at all and what was it all for? Christ knows!

It began to drizzle with rain, which was refreshing on their faces and hands. They hadn't washed for days and their underclothing was filthy from sweat and dried bodily functions that they hadn't noticed in moments of absolute fear and panic. They lifted their heads towards the sky and let the rain trickle down their faces into their mouths. They were hungry and the want for food hit them with a vengeance.

"Jesse?"

"Yeah?"

"I shit myself when we were out there"

"Don't worry mate, guess we all did"

Dead men don't have appetites, so the pair started searching in back packs for anything edible that the rats hadn't yet discovered.

Between them, they shared four hard biscuits and a piece of stale fruitcake, still wrapped in brown paper and probably baked by a loving mother somewhere back in England. There was very little water left in any of the canteens they'd picked up but their thirst was quenched and they collected a few rounds of ammunition, 'just in case.'

It was very quiet now except for some occasional firing in the far off distance. Tired and exhausted they started the walk back, just hoping they were heading in the right direction, listening for any sounds of snipers that might still be combing the woods. They were passed feeling the pain from blisters long since broken on their feet or the sores that had formed where their stiff and dried out clothing was chaffing against their skin. They both had cuts and grazes on their faces and arms and their uniforms were tattered. They'd long since taken off their tunic jackets and back packs so goodness knows where they had left them but Jesse knew Mill's photo was safely in his back trouser packet. He put his hand over his pocket to make sure it was still there. Picking up their riffles they stumbled on, pausing every few moments to listen.

When they came to open ground they decided to crawl on the stomachs keeping as low as they could in fear of being seen. Luck was with them as the moon went behind a cloud,

"Come on mate let's head towards those trees and make a dash for it" Jesse said in a quiet whisper as he nodded towards what appeared to be a small wood a hundred yards or so further ahead, "and if yer believe there's a God up there then yer better start praying. Right! Come on, let's go!"

Weary and fatigued as they were they had to make it to the trees and safety for they were crossing what was known as 'no man's land' German's one side and the British the other. Just two gunshots would send them to their maker. Several corpses lay face down, probably shot in the back as they tried to get back to their lines. If Frank did say a prayer then it was answered because they made it just before the moon came from behind the cloud giving light to the ground they had just covered.

They rested for a while and then started off again. All they wanted to do was sleep but guessed they couldn't be far from their own trenches and carried on.

After a while they came to a clearing and in the moonlight saw the remains of a dead horse and the stench of decaying flesh filled their nostrils. Dozens of rodents scattered as they approached but they didn't see the blue bottles and maggots, which were oblivious of the two intruders.

There was no sign of the rider until Frank noticed the remains of him hanging from a nearby tree where he'd been blown by the enemies' blast. He grabbed hold of Jesse's arm, "Oh God Jesse, just look at that poor bugger up there"

In the moonlight it looked eerie and unreal but it didn't sicken them anymore, it was just another way to die, another way to die in a living nightmare.

They were just moving on when lying in their path were two large bundles which at first Jesse thought were dismembered torsos. They'd seen so many before but somehow these looked different; he went closer to look. The bundles were dirty canvas bags stiff with mud and splattered with blood. There was a length of rope tying the two together; he turned one over with his boot.

He couldn't believe what he was seeing, "Bloody hell! It's only the mail bags!" he cried, He could just make out the 'Queen's Royal West Surrey's 2nd. Batt' stamped on both bags.

"Frank look! It's only our bloody mail!" he exclaimed excitely, "It's our bloody mail!"

How the hell did they get out here? Tired and drained as he was, he realised they must be nearer to their base than they realised and the poor sod in the tree must have been on his way to take the letters to the 'Queen's'.

"Christ, Jess, how come they weren't destroyed along with the horse"

"Lord above knows! Come on mate, let's get this lot back to base, there might be something in it for us."

With the thought that out there in the middle of Kingdom Come, there could be a letter from Mill with news of home he knew they had to get the sacks back.

Suddenly with a burst of new found energy and renewed spirits, they dragged the bags between them over the next four hundred yards and reached the British lines and sanctuary.

It was the 2nd Highland Gordon's that spotted them approaching and a shout went out,

"Here's another two coming in!"

When the men saw them struggling with the mail bags they eagerly came forward to help.

Jesse and Frank sank wearily and exhausted to the ground and when they got their breath back explained how they had found the mail bags.

A private sitting nearby told them they'd got their mail two days before and guessed the poor sod now hanging from a tree was on the way to the Queen's when he'd copped it.

One of the Gordon's called over,

"Get yourselves down here, have some grub and a get a good rest."

The exhausted pair did as they were bid.

Before Jesse knew it he was in a sound sleep and never woke until several hours later. The first thing he noticed when he opened his eyes was a letter lying by his side. Frank must have looked in amongst the others and found it for him.

When he saw Mill's handwriting he cried, he cried as he'd never cried before with great gulping sobs. How he longed to be home, to see his daughters and to walk freely along the streets of London. He longed for the 'Smoke' and the life he had once known. He wanted to sleep in clean sheets and eat real wholesome food and most of all, he wanted to see Mill.

"You alright mate?" someone asked,

"Yeah", he managed to say, "just wanna get 'ome like the rest of us".

He read Mill's letter and was just about to reread it again when two high ranking officers walked into the dug-out where he had lain asleep. A cold feeling swept through his body. 'Oh God!' he thought, 'Christ, they're going to 'ave us for desertion' He felt fear rising in his chest and his heart began to thump in panic. His mind went back to the two Officers who had urged him and Frank to charge towards the oncoming mass of Germans and no doubt to a certain death.

Had these been the same two men? Jesse wouldn't have recognised them if they were, when you're running for your life you don't stop to look at faces. Even if they were the same two, how did they get back then he wondered?

He and Frank who had been sitting with him in the dug-out both stood to attention and saluted as the first Officer spoke,

"At ease men"

"Yes Sir!" they both replied in unison.

"Was there any Hun out there in no man's land?"

Jesse thought they couldn't be the same two men or they wouldn't be asking but maybe they'd got away while they were in the shell hole? Thoughts were racing through his mind.

"We heard them Sir, we could hear them shouting and then shooting our men, they were searching for them in the woods, poor buggers had no chance, no chance at all, shooting them as they found them, one by one."

Jesse wasn't bothered about his language; he was too past it all to care, 'probably going to Court Marshall us anyway' he thought 'cos, they will want to know how we got back alive, what a bloody way to treat your own men'

"Out- numbered by hundreds we were, just a handful of us against that lot and now most of our blokes are out there lying dead and being eaten by the fucking rats! With anger in his voice he cried, "And what the bloody hell was it for, tell me, what the bloody hell was it for?"

He clenched his fists and shook them, he was past caring, "Young blokes still wet behind the ears being told to charge and they did, yes, they did, they went forward bravely to their deaths and as they lay dying in agony they were screaming for their mothers. They were bloody heroes alright but what yer going to tell 'em back 'ome? Died for their country or died screaming for their ma's?"

He sat down and buried his head in his hands and began to weep.

For a moment the Officers stared at the two filthy and bedraggled soldiers. Then the second one who until now had said nothing, "You did a good job bringing that mail back, just what your bunch needs for some moral support. Well done, both of you, Have a bit to eat and some coffee then get yourself and the wee laddie back to your regiment. They're at Bazentin-le-Grand and it's that way", he said pointing out the direction, "and good luck!"

"Thank you Sir!" Jesse stood up and saluted the Officers,

Was that it? Thank God they weren't going to be Court marshalled for disobeying an order, he couldn't believe they were turning a blind eye for they must have had some idea of what had happened.

For many years to come he would suffer dreadful moments of deep depression thinking of those young men who had followed the command and were shot to pieces. Maybe it was guilt but he had followed his natural instincts that had been in him since a young kid on the London streets...to survive one way or another he had to survive.

 They did as they were bid and had a bite to eat in the field kitchen then grabbing the mailbags the pair were soon off.

"Blimey Jesse, we were lucky there, I thought they were having us" "Yeah so did I mate, so did I". After an hour or so they saw a small group of men ahead and as they got nearer excited shouts were heard, "Christ they've got the mail bags! They've got the mail!"

Jesse saw some familiar faces and there was a lot of back slapping and handshaking.

"Are there any more of you?" someone asked.

"No, just us, where's all the rest then?

"Well, so far this lot here is all we've got left," the solider said, gesturing to those who had made it back.

Jesse Warren and Frank who had kept together throughout that terrible ordeal were the last two to come back alive.

Later in the day they received orders to go back to Bray- le-Somme for rest and recovery. For now the fighting was over for the Queen's Royal West Surrey's. Well at least until Saturday 26th August when they were told to prepare for further action.

Jesse dreaded the thought; he could not go through all that again. He'd had enough, his chest was giving him pain and he was having terrible nightmares. He would wake screaming when the dreadful scenes he had witnessed came to haunt him over and over again. He saw men being swallowed alive by the mud, he saw some without legs hanging from trees and torn limbs everywhere.

Bodies entangled in the wire struggling to get free before the snipers finished them and the blood! Every night, night after night he saw the blood. He saw the two brothers who died in each other's arms and the mother who came to them. Sometimes in these living nightmares he saw his mother, Mary Ann and called to her, but she never answered him.

It was the rats you see, the rats that kept her away and the lice. Great big lice, gnawing at his arms, his legs and crawling all over his body. Screaming men would stretch their arms out towards him as they slowly burnt to death in roaring flames. Their blackened faces would smile at him as he walked on a carpet of dead baked flesh. Then he would see John Samuels his old mate, siting in the Greyhound Pub having a drink with Mill and Hetty in the Snug, but John couldn't find his mouth, he had no head.

Sweating and shaking, his own screams would wake him from this torment as he struggled for breath. How could he go back to the front line? Just thinking of it made him start shaking and he felt the palpitations of his heart.

It was 28th August and Jesse was sitting with a few men waiting to receive further orders for the return to the front on the following day. He was physically sick with fear and dread and could not stop the shaking that was now affecting him constantly. "No, I can't go back! I can't go back!", he kept saying over and over again. He sat with his head in his hands. One of his comrades gave him a nudge, "Better stand up Warren, we've got visitors"

Their Lieutenant was walking towards them with a Catholic Priest. The men jumped up and stood to attention.

"Any Catholics here?" the Lieutenant asked.

"No Sir", came a few mumbled replies.

"Pity" said the Officer; the Father here needs a Batman. Jesse saw his chance; he pulled himself up to his full height of 5' 2.5" "I'm a Catholic Sir!"

"Can you ride a horse?" the Padre asked. "Yes Sir!"

"Right then Warren", said the Officer, "get your gear and be back here in ten minutes!" "Yes Sir!" Jesse didn't really know what religion he was, he'd got married in a Church of England and had put that on his signing up form but if the Padre wanted a Catholic to assist him, then a Catholic he was. As for riding a horse well, the nearest he'd ever been to one was seeing them pulling a load as they passed in the streets back home!

And so Jesse became a Batman to a Catholic Priest who introduced himself as Father Bernard Scholfield.

He'd watched the way the priest mounted his horse and Jesse did likewise. He soon got the hang of it and was overjoyed at his stroke of luck, no more marching and hopefully no more fighting. He went with the priest to the field hospitals and stood by while he gave blessings and the Last Rites to the dying. Together they would go out to the screaming men who had fallen in the line of fire as the battles continued and drag back the injured and those who were suffering from convulsions and choking on the deadly poison gases the Germans were using against the British.

There was often no hope for many and the only comfort was to be given a prayer to send them on their way and a few words as they were taken from this world to hopefully, a far better place where they would be at peace. Jesse always offered an 'Amen' and the sign of the cross as the Priest prayed over the dying and was relieved to see their suffering end.

Often he and Father Bernard would throw themselves to the ground as shells and gunfire passed over their heads. Then up and onwards they went, out and to those poor buggers with their faces blown away beyond recognition, some with limbs hanging from sinews or their innards turned inside out. Those that were alive were dragged back and carried off to the First Aid Stations and then on to the overflowing field hospitals and some if lucky, were eventually sent back home to England.

Some poor sods were appallingly disfigured, some had suffered burns or were missing limbs, some were blinded and many were still gasping from the result of chlorine gas inhalation and would suffer for the rest of their lives, many had lost their hearing but yes, they *were* the lucky ones, at least they would have a chance back in England.

But what about those pitiful souls whose faces or what was left of them were so badly disfigured that they were unrecognisable, many unable to speak, see or hear, their identity unknown. Sadly they could not be sent back to their own homes because no one knew who they were although in some cases where the identity was known, families were lead to believe they had been killed in action rather than see the horrendous injuries and sufferings of their men folk who had fought so bravely for their country. They were taken to a special hospital somewhere in the heart of the English countryside and spent the rest of their remaining days there.

The unlucky ones were those who made a good recovery and were ordered back yet again to the front line and each time their chances of survival grew less.

Both Jesse and Father Bernard were now in poor health themselves. The fumes from the chlorine gas on the men they carried back were often inhaled and they would vomit and cough until they fell exhausted. But it had to be done and time and time again they went back with little protection from the deadly poison.

Jesse always attended Mass with all the able bodied men and often wondered what Mill would think if she knew he had become a Catholic although as he told himself he would be only for the 'duration' but he knew in his heart there was little chance of him ever getting out of this stinking hell but he thanked God he was still alive.

Over the next four months he got to know Father Bernard Schofield very well. Jesse learnt that he too had come from London and had entered the church in 1903. He'd been ordained in 1910 in the Servite church of St. Mary's, the Priory in Fulham Road and that he had resided there ever since.

Father Bernard was several years older than Jesse and was in France for one year's service as was common practice with men of most religious denominations. Once when sitting during a quiet moment when no firing was heard and men were resting, Father Bernard told Jesse how he'd had his tonsils removed just as he was due to leave England and he's Service in France had to be delayed. 'I thought having my tonsils out was bad enough' the priest had said 'but it was nothing compared to this bloody lot'. That was the only time Jesse had heard the man swear.

In the November Father Bernard was released from service and given papers to return home to Fulham. Jesse was sorry to see him go although he wished him well but he would have given anything to be going with him and home to Mill.

"Don't need a Batman back in the Priory then?" Jesse joked with the priest.

"If only I did" he replied, "I'll see what I can do" he jested.

The priest thanked Jesse for his service and gave him a Blessing. He promised to keep in touch when it was all over. 'Much chance of that' thought Jesse but he would always have respect for any Catholic he ever met up with and as he went to ride away the priest hesitated turned and said,

"Oh, by the way Warren," he paused for a moment, "you're not a Catholic are you?"

"No Sir," Jesse replied truthfully.

"And you'd never ridden a horse before, had you?"

Once again Jesse answered truthfully, "No Sir".

The Padre smiled, saluted him and rode away.

Later that day Jesse heard news of the Queen's. They had gone back to the front lines after new replacements had been drafted in from England and then forward to the edge of Delville Wood and on to Hop Alley. But then they were attacked again and once more suffered greatly. The following day they went along the eastern edge of Delville Wood, which had proved to be a success, and hid up with the 8th Devonshire's. A day of sniping and shelling followed and on the 7th again the Queen's attacked the eastern corner of Delville Wood. More and more men had fallen, some only being in France a few days. This attack failed and the exhausted men had been relieved by the 55th Division. Jesse was told to prepare for more active duty the following morning. The pain in his chest was making breathing difficult and his head was hurting, he needed to sit down but orders were being shouted at him to march forward and then blackness came over him in waves and as he staggered forward he passed out.

Chapter Eight

The sound of rustling by his side woke Jesse from a fretful sleep. It was the rats, he had to get rid of the rats, he could hear them moving about. He wanted to open his eyes, but they felt so heavy and his head was hurting. It felt as if a tight steel band was around it and pains shot across his eyes. His chest was hurting as he breathed and panic set in as he struggled to move...... He had to get rid of the rats!

Someone was holding his hand and he heard a woman's voice whisper softly, "Hush now Jesse, just take it easy".

The rats had gone; he couldn't hear them any more.

He tried opening his eyes again and through a grey mist saw a young woman standing there dressed in white. A cool hand soothed his troubled brow. Jesse thought he must be dead and his Mother was with him. He knew she would come one day; he had been waiting for her. He hadn't wanted to die but he had known his chances of surviving grew less and less as another day passed. His thoughts went to Mill and he closed his eyes again.

"Mum, tell Mill I'm sorry, Oh, Mill I'm so sorry, tell her mum, tell her for me" He had done his best and had really tried to stay alive, but he was so tired, "I'm so sorry Mill", he murmured as he drifted back to sleep.

He woke again when he heard voices. The mist was clearing but he couldn't understand where he was or what was happening. Someone asked how he felt, but he couldn't answer. The woman was standing there again this time with a board in her hand and making notes. A man in a white opened coat over khaki uniform was holding his wrist with two fingers on his pulse. It seemed like a hospital but he couldn't remember being in hospital and was puzzled, he thought he had died. He was sure he had seen Mary Ann, his mother. He wasn't lying on the rough churned up earth of the battlefields so he could only be in Heaven.

"Where am I?" he asked in a hoarse whisper "where's my mother? Am I dead?"

"By all accounts you should be after what you've been through," it was the man in the white coat who was speaking, "but no, you're not dead, you're in hospital and against all odds you're still alive Warren. There won't be any more fighting son, you've done your bit"

Sheer utter relief swept over him and he tried to ask more questions, but he was very, very tired and was told to just take it easy and rest.

He had very little memory of what had happened. He recalled the absolute fear and terror he'd felt when he'd been ordered to assemble with the new batch of Queen's to go back to the front line but after that everything seemed hazy and confused.

Many times he had drifted in and out of his nightmares and often woke screaming. The woman who he'd thought had been his mother came to comfort him and bathed his fevered head and perspiring body in cool water. He had vague memories of being prompted to swallow soup of some sort, being washed and sitting in a chair. Sometimes he was walking up and down, back and forth, was it in the trenches? He felt confused; he hadn't known where it was. At first he wasn't convinced that the rustling noise he had often heard was the starched uniform of a nurse and not the rats scampering along the trenches ready to feast on the dead and dying. Clean linen felt wonderful against his skin and Jesse sighed contentedly as he realised the lice were no longer biting into his flesh. He'd got so used to it but now, like the rats, they were gone. For the first time in many months he felt clean.

Gradually as he began to regain his strength, flashbacks of memory slowly returned and he tried to piece things together. He remembered getting ready for the return to the front and how he had suddenly began shaking and hadn't been able to move. Pain had been shooting through his chest and he'd heard loud rushing noises in his ears. He recalled his legs giving way under him but it was blank after that. Then later a beach came to mind and Jesse thought about it. He saw himself digging the sand with the butt of his rifle and then burying the gun.

'Why would I want to do that?' he asked himself.

Suddenly he remembered; he'd vowed that never again would he shoot another man and in disgust of the whole rotten war and what he had endured wanted to be rid of his weapon. Without a gun he couldn't kill and he never wanted to see it again.

Between bouts of sleeping, reliving his nightmares and waking in cold sweats he remembered things. He thought there had been a ship and someone had been playing a mouth organ and he'd heard the groaning of injured men. He had vague memories of a loud cheer going up and then climbing into the back of a wagon. Father Bernard was with him, talking in a kind whisper or was it just delirium? He seemed to have just snatches of memory, but yes, he was sure Father Bernard was there.

It occurred to him that if he had been on a ship then he had crossed water. Was he back in England? He felt his heart beat faster at the thought, could he really be back home?

The nurse came to check his pulse. He opened his eyes and looked at her. The grey mist had cleared and he saw she was a pretty little thing wearing the uniform of the Queen Alexander Auxiliary Nurses.

"Well", she said smiling at him, "it's nice to see you back with us Jesse Warren".

"Where....where am I?" he was almost afraid to ask, "Am I in England?"

"You certainly are," she replied, "you're well away from the trenches now," she paused and then lent over and whispered in his ear, "You're in Manchester and you won't be going back to France".

Jesse could hardly believe his ears! It was true, he was home in England but what on earth was he doing in Manchester? Even though he wasn't really sure what had happened or how he'd got there, he was home at last. Unashamedly the tears rolled down his cheeks

"What happened?" he asked the nurse. "How did I get 'ere"

She told him that he had been completely exhausted, mentally and physically and he was no longer fit enough to be in a fighting regiment and had been sent home to England. "Thank God for that" He would rather have died then go through all that again.

He was amazed when he learnt that he had been in the hospital for almost six weeks and that it was nearly Christmas.

"What year?" he jokingly asked the nurse.

She smiled and said,

"It's still 1916"

"Does my wife know I'm here?" he asked.

"Yes, she would have been notified and I believe there is a letter for you" she replied opening the drawer of the bedside cupboard.

Jesse eagerly read the letter from Mill. In it she thanked God for his safe return and had wanted to come to see him but he was to have no visitors while still in the state of shock. She and the girls were well and they hoped he would be home for Christmas. He was to look after himself and they were awaiting his homecoming. She had put two kisses from young Milly and Cissy.

He was glad she hadn't tried to make the long journey for he wouldn't have wanted her to see the state he must have been in when they brought him back.

With dedicated care, his health had slowly improved. He still had nightmares and the doctor told him that there was nothing they could do about that,

"They may pass in time," he had said, "it is still very early days yet, but think how very lucky you are compared to some of these poor blighters. They may never recover."

Jesse looked around the hospital ward. There were about twenty other beds.

Yes, he was lucky. He was beginning to understand now. Some of the men sat rocking backwards and forwards; two were huddled in a corner with their hands over their ears as if trying to protect themselves from the noise of the shelling and bombing.

Another thought he still had his machine gun and was going through the actions of firing it while sitting up in bed. One or two were trying to read books but Jesse could see their hands trembling. He thought of all the thousands laying dead back in the battlefields whose bodies would never be recovered and yes, he knew he was very, very lucky indeed.

Christmas came and went, but Jesse was not allowed home.

"Give it another couple of weeks", the Doctor had told him when Jesse asked if he could have leave.

He was disappointed, because he wanted to get back to Mill and his family, but he knew he needed time to adjust.

How would they feel about each other when he got back? How would she cope with the nightmares? What would Mill think if he started screaming out during the night? Would their lives ever be the same? Would he be able to live with the horror of what he had experienced?

He suddenly remembered the young sixteen-year-old who had stayed with him throughout those terrible days. They had said a quick goodbye before Jesse left with the Catholic Priest and had wished each other luck and hoped to meet up again when he got back. Jesse would have taken him too, but it wasn't possible and sadly he never had a chance to find out what had happened to him

He hoped the lad had got through. Even when they had both been terrified out of their lives Frank had kept going and Jesse wondered if he himself would have given up had he been out in that wood alone. There were times when he felt it impossible to go on any more but the two of them had kept each other going. For as long as he lived he would never forget the bravery of that young boy and hoped that they would meet again sometime but it wasn't to be for Jesse never saw him again.

A few days after Christmas Jesse was quite surprised to receive a letter from Father Bernard. 'Well, the old boy didn't forget me after all' Jesse mused to himself. The letter was just a short note asking after him and hoping that he received the letter as all he knew was that Jesse had been sent to a Manchester hospital. Jesse read it over several times and began to recall snatches of the journey on the ship. 'Had Father Bernard been with him?' he wondered 'had he any part in getting him back?' Jesse had little recollection of what happened the day after the Priest left for England. In his heart he knew that Father Bernard must have helped him and somehow got him home. Jesse vowed then that he would also remember the kindness of that man until his own dying day. There would be a lot to remember and a lot to forget.

He was given a blue uniform known as 'Army Blues' to show that he was no longer on active service abroad and had been hospitalised. He also had and a ten-day furlough. He knew he would still be in the army but was being transferred to the Labour Corps and the newly formed Royal Flying Corps at Nottingham. "Christ!" did they think he was going up in one of those machines flying through the air?" He had even been given a new serial number but he guessed he would be keeping his feet firmly on the ground.

 He had hoped that he would be discharged, but being he had since made a good recovery from his ordeals in France and Belgium, he was considered fit enough to continue in Service. At least he would be in this country and hopefully have opportunities to get home now and again.

He vowed never to leave the shores of England again and throughout his lifetime he never did.

How long this war would continue was anyone's guess. The 'Big Push' they had talked about so long ago which had eventually taken place on 1st July the previous year had been meant to finish it all, but instead of Victory, 70,000 men lost their lives on that first fateful day alone. The Germans had dug themselves well in and the majority had survived the six-day bombardment in their deep concrete shelters. But still the battle had gone on for over four months until the 20th November.

127, 751 good brave men were now dead. 49, 000 were never identified; and many were classed as 'missing'. Jesse knew only too well what this meant; he'd seen so many men blown to 'Kingdom Come' and had just simply disappeared.

His thoughts were with the Queen's still out there and he knew of the atrocities those who had survived were still going through. He had enough memories of what he'd seen to last him a life time and he knew those memories would haunt him for as long as he lived.

Jesse had made his way to 'The Smoke' and was now on the train heading towards St. James Street station in Walthamstow. Mill knew he was coming home but didn't know exactly when it would be and had no idea he was already on his way.

When he'd been released from hospital, there hadn't been time to write, he'd just grabbed his gear and caught the next London bound train.

It was absolutely wonderful to be back. The air was as thick as ever and it was snowing, just like the day he had left on the February morning so long ago. Jesse knew exactly how long it had been, two years all but one month. From the 15th February 1915 to the 15th, January 1917. He had only seen Mill and the girls for a brief visit before he went to France and was feeling nervous about seeing them again.

The train had been packed with weary and worn out soldiers at Liverpool Street and many had to stand but none cared..... they were heading home! Gradually the carriages emptied as the train pulled into stations along the line.

It halted at Bethnal Green, the station Jesse had left from just days after he had joined up and two more soldiers got up to leave,

"All the best mate!" they called as they slung their kit bags over their backs.

There was only one chap left in the carriage now and Jesse asked where he was heading,

"Hoe Street mate," the chap replied hesitantly just as the guard came along slamming the heavy doors that the soldiers had left open.

As their door banged shut the man jumped and suddenly began shaking uncontrollably. His boots were banging on the floor and saliva began to dribble from the corner of his mouth. Sweat began pouring down his face.

Jesse lent across had patted him on the knee,

"Come on mate" he said trying to comfort the man, "yer be O.K."

He had seen this happen to so many men who had been out in the front lines and in the hospital. Maybe that's how he'd been himself? He couldn't remember.

The train began to move on.

"How….can…can… I… go….home….like this?" the shaking man asked Jesse. "What…what will…they fink…of…me?"

"They won't fink nothing mate" Jesse answered trying to reassure the man, "Just you get 'ome mate and have a bloody good rest, that's what yer need."

He talked to the poor fellow until the train stopped at St. James Street Station and wished his companion good luck. He was thankful that he himself had made a good recovery and hadn't been left like this poor sod.

"See yer around mate" Jesse said as he opened the carriage door and tried not to slam it as he got off.

He came out of the station and turned right into Courtney place. Just a few yards along to his right an alley way went under the railway and continued into Side Road. Jesse followed this, crossing Brunner Road and came out into Southgrove Road. He stopped for a moment on the corner where the roads met to inhale the wonderful smell coming from the Essex Brewery Tap just along the road to the right. It had been so long since he tasted a pint of real English beer and promised himself that treat for the following day. He was pleased to know that the brewery was still producing even though the country was at war.

He turned left and began marching along Southgrove towards Gosport Road, passing Cranbrook Road where Mill's mother and family lived. He couldn't get out of the habit of marching; it was second nature to him. He carried on until he came to Gosport Road at the top and crossed into Netley Road. It was late afternoon and already dark, the snow crunched underfoot, but Jesse didn't feel the cold. Far from it, he was beginning to sweat as his heart started beating faster; he was nearly there and at long, long last nearly home. He felt excited but apprehensive and began to tremble.

He looked at the numbers on the doors and knew that 61 was about a hundred yards down on the left. He was getting near, 55...57....59, then as he approached the next house he stopped and hesitated,

'What do I say to her?' he wondered and stood for a moment by the gate.

'Would the girls remember him?' He knew little Cissy wouldn't, but young Milly might.

There were now only a few feet between him, the front door and his family whom he had not seen for such a long, long time. It was like crossing from one life into another, something he had so often dreamed about and that's what had kept him going throughout those terrible days and nights.

Tears were streaming down his face; he couldn't believe that he was really home, that he'd got back safe. He thought of John his mate from Bethnal Green and wondered how Hetty was. Mill had written to say she'd heard from her and sadly John had been killed on the first day of that terrible battle on the Somme. He would go and see her before he went back.

He thought of Gratton Houses where it had all began. He remembered how he had gone to join up because there was no other way to keep Mill and the girls from starving. He shook his head and smiled to himself as he recalled thinking that it would probably be just for a few weeks and the war would be over. How wrong they all were, they'd said it would be finished by Christmas 1914 and here he was, still in uniform at the start of 1917.

Would anyone want to know what had happened out there and if they did, would they believe it? He very much doubted it. No one could ever imagine what it had been like unless they had gone through it themselves no, never in a million years could they have imagined what it was like.

Taking a deep breath he walked up to the door. He hadn't wanted Mill to see him crying but now he just didn't care, he was back; he'd made it back against so many odds. He nervously lifted the knocker and banged it down.

A few seconds later a light went on in the passage and shone through the skylight window above the door. His heart was thumping in his chest, his palms were sweating.

Mill opened the door desperately hoping and praying that it would be Jesse and then when she saw him standing there, she threw herself into his arms. No words were spoken, their tears and sobs mingled together as they clung to each other. His life had been spared; he had fought in a war that would not only be indescribable but beyond belief. When he'd left Bethnal Green to volunteer nearly two years earlier he had done it for Mill and for his children but then with thousands of other young men like himself, they fought for their King and their country but it was for the love of Amelia he had taken the King's Shilling.

END OF PART ONE

He took the King's Shilling

FOR THE LOVE OF AMELIA

Part 2

Continuing the story of

Mill and Jesse Warren and how it all came about.

By their granddaughter

Marion Cunningham

Mill c. 1912

Jesse in Army blues c.1918

*Mill with young Milly (left) and Cissy
c.1918*

*Mill and Jesse with Milly, Vera and Cissy
c.1920*

Chapter One

On the 14th July 1888 Sarah Elizabeth Herod (formerly Shipley) gave birth to a daughter. She was the first child born to Sarah and her husband Joseph. Sarah was just 18 and Joseph five years older. They decided to name the child Amelia Charlotte, Amelia after Sarah's own mother and Charlotte after Joseph's mother. The young couple were living in Hoxton Old Town, East London at the time and Joseph was employed as a Cellar man in a local Public House. However, he had always wanted to better himself and one night in the pub he overheard talk of properties being built by the hundreds for the working classes a few miles away in Walthamstow.

He had just brought two crates of Ben Trumann's up from the cellar when he'd heard a couple of burley Irish navies who were leaning on the bar, discussing their prospects. One was saying that he reckoned there would be work there for at least a couple of years and suggested to his mate that they both went the following morning to see about getting a job.

Joseph had no building experience but hearing this he thought maybe there would be a chance of getting some work there himself. They were bound to be needing labourers if that many houses were being built and decided he would make a trip to Walthamstow as soon as he could and see what his chances were. If he struck lucky and the pay was better than the pittance he was earning now then he would take Sarah and his new daughter Amelia, whose name had already been shortened to Mill, out of Hoxton Old Town and move over to Walthamstow.

He made some inquiries and heard that a company by the name of Malcolm Macleod & Co Ltd. were taking on casual labourers. Rows and rows of two up and two down back to back houses were being erected and yes, more labour was needed. He had no skills but was willing to take on any work offered and feeling optimistic went along to the yard in Glen Road where he applied for a job. His luck was in, he was taken on and although he didn't know it then, he was to stay with that company for the next 30 years.

Macleod's was a concrete company that made the stone door-steps, window ledges and lintels for the numerous houses that were being built in the area. Concrete was in great demand so business was flourishing and Glen Road was in the middle of the numerous streets that were rapidly appearing all around. Nearby in Selbourne Road, were the brick fields. The colossal amounts of bricks made there day after day were used to create the housing boom that was quickly rising in this part of Walthamstow.

Joseph soon found a house that had a couple of rooms to let and within two weeks, when Amelia was just a babe in arms they moved into rented accommodation just off the busy High Street at no.1, Buxton Road.

Sarah was pleased to move away from Hoxton Old Town because just three miles away in Whitechapel women were being brutally murdered by a man who was to become known as the notorious Jack the Ripper. She shuddered at the thought of such horrendous crimes and feared he could strike anywhere, even within their area. So yes, she was certainly pleased that they were now living in a new district, especially as the High Street boasted a very extensive market.

It wasn't long before she was pregnant again and by the time their first son James, was born they had moved on again and were now renting a house at 42, South Grove Road on the other side of the High Street and within a few minutes' walk to Glen Road and Macleod's.

It was here in South Grove Road that another son, Joseph and then Beatrice their second daughter were born and it was also here that James died of fright when he was just two years old. The child was lying ill in bed with measles when a monkey which had escaped from his master, an organ grinder, had shinned the outside drain-pipe and jumped through an open window onto the sleeping child. The death was recorded as convulsions although it was always said it was the shock that was the true cause of this young child's demise.

It wasn't long after this incident that Joseph and his family moved once again, this time to nearby Cranbrook Road which was a short turning with recently built back to back houses on either side. First they lived at no. 13 and Joseph also rented no.15 (why no one can say for sure) but when their third daughter Lydia was born they moved along the road to no.25 giving up the other two properties. This was to be their last move because they remained in this house for the rest of their lives. Sarah was giving birth almost on a yearly basis until there were eventually fifteen offspring. It was said that counting miscarriages and still births her pregnancies had actually totalled 23 in 25 years! Two or possibly three children died in infancy and because of the lack of good nourishing food at least one daughter, Lydia, had rickets which caused her to have very bandy legs throughout her life. As the family increased in size they still continued to live in this small back to back house that only had two rooms upstairs, two downstairs and a back scullery. To accommodate this large brood, as many as possible slept sideways across two double beds in each of the upstairs rooms and the younger ones slept in with Sarah and Joseph. I feel a great compassion for Sarah my great grandmother, there was no form of contraception and these numerous pregnancies no doubt were conceived when Joseph came home drunk on a Saturday night and demanded his 'rights'. Now in the 21st Century you may ask, "Why on earth did women put up with this?"

The answer is simply because that's how life was, there was no choice and if a woman did object then a husband who was full of drink could easily become violent and thought nothing of giving his wife a beating. Nowadays it would be classed as rape and assault but in those days big families were the normal thing and understandably women were tired and worn out long before their time. Many died in childbirth and it was no surprise that the infant mortality was very high. The first thing parents usually did after the birth of a baby and providing they could somehow manage the weekly instalments, was to take out insurance on the new born child. If the child did not survive at least the cost of a funeral would be covered, if not then they would be buried in a paupers grave or in some cases the baby would be placed in a coffin with a deceased person about to have a private burial. In those early days when Sarah had married Joseph it meant she now belonged to her husband and the word 'Obey' in the marriage vows meant exactly that. She had no rights, there was no woman's refuge or help, she had to do as he said and Sarah like so many woman of that era just accepted it as a way of life. She had made her own bed and just had to lie on it. Men considered them to be their 'property'. Women didn't even have the vote and many only married for some form of security although in some cases they thought marriage would be a wonderful and happy love match, for some perhaps it was. Many came from abusive homes and saw marriage as a way to escape but were soon very disillusioned and more often than not ended up in an even worst situation. Sex in marriage was a man's right and obviously there was no consideration for a wife being continuously pregnant or any thought as to how these children would be fed let alone clothed. This was a very selfish attitude and Joseph was no different or maybe he just didn't know any better?

Sarah had learnt to read and write when she was younger and had been working in a sweet factory when she'd meet

Sarah and Joseph Herod
Wedding day July 1888

Sarah and Joseph c.1935

Joseph Herod (marked with a cross) France W.W.1

Joseph. However, finding herself pregnant with his child they had hastily married on 16th May 1888. Mill was born two months later.

Joseph had previously joined the Old Tower Hamlets in 1885 that later became The City of London Volunteers which then went on to became the 1st/4th City of London Royal Fusiliers. It may have been that he had been away serving or training with his regiment and had returned home to find Sarah with child and had married quickly. Although Sarah was able to sign their marriage certificate with a flourish, Joseph could only add X as his mark.

Life became very hard for Mill for being the eldest child she was expected to take on a great deal of the responsibility where the raising and caring for this very large brood was concerned. Looking after the younger ones and helping with the washing, ironing, cooking, bathing plus feeding the smaller ones kept Mill very busy and the work was tiring and exhausting. As her sisters grew older they too had to do their share but most of the work fell onto Mill.

However, somehow she was fortunate to have had some schooling and could read and write (unlike her father) and was in fact very bright. As she grew older she'd got work as a machinist in a nearby shirt factory but every penny she earned had to go to help with keeping her younger brothers and sisters clothed and fed. It was a very difficult time and money was short even with Joseph working but a lot of his money went on beer and tobacco, which was again a man's right. It didn't matter if his wife and children went short on food nor had shoes on their feet; a man still had to have his beer and baccy money which in most cases came first.

As the years passed most of the older children were working although they were only receiving a low wage. They were poorly educated and had little skills. The other younger ones who weren't working helped with the household chores. It didn't help matters when Sarah found that once again she was pregnant and so with yet another mouth to feed she decided to take in a paying lodger.

Mill, now 22 years old was not only horrified at the thought of yet another child coming into the household but her mother was now advertising for a boarder! Goodness knows where he or she would sleep. No doubt it would be a man because no woman would want to move it with that lot so a new lodger would have to either bunk in with the boys, sleep in the scullery or even in the outside privy for all Mill cared.

A day or so later a young man in his early twenties knocked on the front door and asked if the room was still vacant. He was ushered in by Tom, one of Mill's brothers and when he learned that he would have to share a room with several other young men and boys it certainly wasn't quite what he had been expecting. However, he was after all in a hurry to find digs and it wasn't going to cost him an arm and a leg, besides he was used to roughing it and didn't intend to stay in Walthamstow for more than a week.

He explained that he had come from Hoxton Old Town where he lodged with an aunt and that he was a French Polisher by trade. He had the chance of some work in the area and needed somewhere to stay until the job was completed. Sarah was only too pleased to take him in especially when she had learnt that he came from her home town of Hoxton even though she knew Mill her eldest daughter would not be at all happy with the situation.

The young man decided he would stay with the Herod's for the week even though it meant bunking in with the older 'boys' and as he turned to leave the room he bumped into Mill who was on a dinner break from work. The young man introduced himself....... 'I'm Jesse Warren' he said. The year was 1910.

Jesse had taken a shine to Mill and came back to stay with the Herod's whenever he had a job on in Walthamstow.

Slowly over the following months they got to know each other better and became friends. Jesse could see what life was like for her and knew Sarah would never let him 'walk out' with Mill because she was needed too much at home and besides, Sarah had given birth to another child since he had been staying there, giving Mill another one to help care for. In fact there were so many children in this household that Jesse had long since given up trying to remember their names and just who was who.

As it was, Jesse did pluck up the courage to ask Mill if she would like to come to visit his aunt in Hoxton for Sunday tea. Much to his amazement Sarah allowed Mill to make this trip, probably because she did not want to upset her lodger who was contributing extra cash whenever he stayed with them, which was becoming more frequent as time passed. And so it was agreed, Mill could go with Jesse for tea at his aunts the following Sunday.

As Mill was putting a hat pin into her best hat and about to leave, her mother warned her not to stay out too late because not only did she have work the following day but it was also washing day. Washing would take the whole of Monday to do and Mill would be expected to get up extra early to help her sisters out before she started work at the factory the following morning.

However, Mill did stay out late in fact she never even came home at all that night. Not that she meant to stay out all night, that was something she wouldn't have dreamed of doing but they had missed the last train and had little choice but to stay with Jesse's aunt and return early the next day.

She'd had such an enjoyable afternoon getting to know Jesse's aunt and then having tea after a walk in the nearby park. They even sang some Music Hall songs around the piano and neighbours came in to join them. Time flew by so quickly and it was only when Mill said she had better leave for home that they realised the trains were restricted on a Sunday.

She certainly wasn't looking forward to having to explain to her mother what had happened and was hoping that Jesse would accompany her back to Walthamstow. However, he had a days work in Cambridge Heath Road the following day and as there wasn't time to go back with her she had no choice but to face her mother's anger alone. After seeing Mill safely onto the train Jesse went on his way, secretly relieved that he didn't have to face Sarah and hoped that by the time he returned to face her which would be that evening, everything would be smoothed over.

As Mill got off the train at James Street Station she dreaded having to face her mother but to her astonishment she didn't have to wait long. For there was Sarah, standing outside the station with her arms folded, still wearing her apron and a look of thunder on her face. "How dare you!" she shouted, "Where the bloody hell have you been all night you little cow!" Mill cringed with fear and embarrassment as other passengers began to turn and stare at the commotion. "But mum….' Mill began as her mother lunged towards her….'I missed the train'.

"Missed the train you little tart!" Sarah cried, "I'll soon give you what for you bloody little liar!" With that she snatched Mill's lovely best black Sunday hat that was adorned with ostrich feathers and pulled it from her head and began hitting her with it.

Mill tried to back away from her mother and the accusations that were being hurled at her and away from the stares of the people who were now gathering to watch what was known in the East End as a right ol' ding dong. "Where does 'is Aunt live? I'll get over there meself and sort 'er out too. And if that Jesse dares to come back 'ere tonight then the boy's will soon sort 'im out" referring to her sons'.

"Yeah!", shouted a voice …'Give 'im wot for luv keeping yer daughter out all night!"

"Bugger off and mind yer own bleeding business" Sarah shouted back to the cries of laughter from the bystanders.

Fearful of her brother's tempers and their willingness to do as their mother bid Mill cried, "Nothing happened, honest mum. We all had a good time and a sing along round the piano and the time just went by and we missed the last train back" Sarah had grabbed Mill by the arm and roughly pulled her …"Where does she live then" she demanded "Tell me!"

"Alright, alright, let go of me, everyone's looking…. its Salisbury Street, Hoxton Old Town"

Sarah let go and just stood staring at Mill, "Where did yer say?"

"I've just told yer, Salisbury Street", Mill was rubbing her arm where Sarah had grabbed her.

"What number Salisbury Street?" she asked, as she seemed to calm down.

"Number 35"

"Are yer having me on girl?"

"No, I'm not, that's where she lives, I told yer, I've only just come from there"

Sarah just stood there for a moment with a look of astonishment on her face and then slowly took a deep breath and said,

'Mill, *that* was the house you were born in, number 35"

Mill knew she had been born in Hoxton Old Town but had no idea where and was shocked at her mother's revelation, "Are yer sure?" she asked

" 'Couse I'm bloody sure I had yer didn't I?"

The crowd started to disperse as mother and daughter stunned at the coincidence began to walk quietly away. By the time they were both back home in Cranbrook Road Sarah's anger had subsided, she was dumbstruck. Of all the roads in Hoxton and of all the houses, Jesse's family were now living in the very same house that she and Joseph had rented when they'd first got married.

When Jesse returned that evening to his relief all was well at number 25 and Sarah who was still finding it hard to believe that such a coincidence could happen, wanted to know all the news of old neighbours and friends whom she had known while living in the same street, let alone the very same house. Jesse told them all that he knew but he too couldn't believe the coincidence either but promised to take Sarah to visit his aunt the next time he and Mill went there for tea. This pleased Sarah and she soon became very fond of Jesse and after that she didn't object to Jesse taking Mill to the Hackney Empire on the odd occasion.

It was soon after this incident that Mill and Jesse decided to get married and a date was set for Christmas Day in St James's Church, Walthamstow.

Sarah did not like the idea of Mill getting married and leaving home, in fact she was against the idea of any of her girls marrying but Mill was now 23 years old and Sarah could do nothing to stop her as much as she protested. It could be she had her own reasons for being against any of them marrying for not only did she need help with the household chores especially with so many at home, there was the wages they contributed including Mill's to think about.

However, apart from the income it could also be said that Sarah may have been trying to protect her daughters from a life such as she'd had herself. With a demanding husband that left her pregnant year in and year out, frequent miscarriages and a life full of drudgery and hardships through having far too many children she may not have wished that fate on her daughters. And if she could prevent the boys from marrying as well then she would. It would stop them from inflicting more women with the same suffering like she had endured for all those years with their own father.

She did partly get her wish as time passed for just two of her sons, Joe and Ernest were the only ones to marry and the rest remained bachelors all their lives.

The year was 1911 when Mill and Jesse married. Joseph, Mill's father was to give the Bride away but because he had been celebrating the forth-coming wedding well in advance he was no longer in a fit state to walk his daughter up the aisle. It was decided that the honour of the occasion should be taken over by her eldest brother Joe who was more than happy to oblige and so they left for the church leaving their father at home to sleep it off. Or so they thought!

There was no money for a traditional wedding dress so instead Mill wore a long ankle length dark grey skirt and a white lace blouse that fitted neatly into her skirt and showed off her trim waist. The blouse had fitted sleeves with frilled cuffs and a wide lace yoke with a high neck, as was the fashion of the day. She had decided against wearing the same hat that her mother had snatched from her head when she had been waiting for her at St James Street Station following her unforgettable visit to meet Jesse's Aunt Amy. Instead she had worn a white lace one that she'd loaned from one of her sisters.

The wedding took place in St. James's the Greater Church not far from Cranbrooke Road and at the junction of Markhouse and St James's Street. Although there was no snow that Christmas Day Mill was to recall that it was windy and cold but they didn't mind, she was starting a new life with Jesse and they both had everything to look forward to. She knew Jesse would be the right man for her and although he liked the odd pint now and again, she felt sure he would never be brutal and violent like her own father could be.

As she walked slowly up the aisle with Joe the sound of the Wedding March began. It wasn't the church organ, they couldn't have afforded that but it sounded more like a mouth organ being played rather badly and way out of tune.

Everyone looked around and although they all guessed who it would be Mill was still dismayed to see that her drunken father who they thought was at home, had entered the church and was swaying unsteadily from side to side. Then just as he began stumbling towards them his knees buckled underneath him and he lurched forward, fell sideways and disappeared between two empty pews.

Sarah was heard muttering in disgust and a general murmur went around the congregation. "Leave 'im there! She hissed as a couple of guests rose to assist him and then quietly under her breath hoping the Vicar didn't hear added, "Drunken ol' bugger"

Being no-one bothered to help him up, there he lay throughout the ceremony, snoring in a drunken stupor.

As Mill turned back and continued towards the alter Joe lent towards her and whispered, "Christ Almighty Mill, I thought this was a going to be a wedding not a bloody funeral, look what Jesse's wearing!"

None of her brothers or guests had a decent suit between them but they had all made an effort for the occasion and wore their Sunday best clothes and had polished their boots. The men carried their caps while the women wore their best hats and some had shawls on account of the weather but Mill gasped when she saw what Jesse had on. Of course she expected him to look his best for their wedding day but how could he turn up looking like that!

He was wearing a black coat with tails, a white stiff high collar and grey pinstriped trousers. He was holding a black silk top hat in his hand and as Mill got closer she noticed there were black silk ribbons hanging from the back.

As she stood beside him she said in a hushed voice, "Blimey Jesse, you look like a bloody undertaker" regardless to whether the Vicar had overheard or not.

"I didn't have a suit" he whispered back, "so I borrowed this from my ol' mate Arthur English".

"But Jesse" exclaimed Mill, "Arthur English *is* an undertaker!" And the Vicar began, 'Dearly beloved…'

It would be ten years before there was another wedding in the Herod household. In 1921 Helen, one of Mill's sisters married but she did so without even telling her mother because she knew Sarah would be against it and there was no way she'd give permission for her to wed.

Helen was 19 at the time and two years below the age of consent. It was never known who had signed the consent form, which was necessary for the Banns to be read and the marriage to take place. Her father Joseph may have learnt to write his name by then as he had only put his mark of an X on his own wedding certificate way back in 1888. It was however suspected that one of the brothers may have had something to do with it but none of them ever owned up to doing it and the wedding had gone ahead without any fuss or celebrations.

When Sarah heard the news that one of her under aged daughters had married that afternoon without her knowledge let alone permission and had also left home to live with a man, regardless of being married, she was absolutely furious. So much so she went and found Helen and dragged her back home despite protests from her and the new bridegroom. Sarah forbade Helen to leave the house and it would be another 3 months before she relented and let her go back to live with her new husband!

Beatrice, Lydia, Edith and Elsie were all to marry but not until they were 21 and even then it was still against Sarah's wishes. However times were changing and big families such as the Herod's were no longer as common as they had been in the past. Any possible fears Sarah may have had concerning her own children producing very large families never materialised for as the years passed she was only blessed with very few grandchildren.

It is hard to believe that with Sarah and Joseph having such a large family including several sons, not one of them would pass on the name of Herod.

Joseph their eldest son had married Emily and they had just one child, a boy also named Joseph. Sadly he died around the age of 20 from complications that set in after an appendix operation and so the chance to carry on the family name died with him. Ernest, another of Mill's brothers who had married only had one child that was a daughter. Joseph and Emily were so distraught at losing their only child that after his death they left the bedroom where he'd slept just as it had been on the day he died. They never moved from that house and although it was dusted, young Joseph's room along with his bicycle and all his personal effects remained untouched until their own deaths many years later.

Meanwhile Jesse had a friend named John Samuels whom he had known from his younger days in Hoxton who was now living in Gratton Houses, a large block of dwellings in Globe Road, Bethnal Green. It was John who had told them of a couple of rooms that were for let and it was here that Mill and Jesse began their married life. My own mother was born in Gratton Houses on January 13th 1913 and although she was always known as 'young' Milly she was Baptised Elizabeth Amelia.

At the outbreak of war in 1914 Joseph, Mill's father re-joined his regiment and spent a long period of time serving in Malta and France mainly as a cook.   Mill's eldest brother Joe who by then was 24 also served in W.W.1 and even met up with his father whilst in France.

It was also from here in Globe Road, Bethnal Green that Jesse Warren walked to enlist in the Army on the 15th April 1915 and from here Mill walked in the snow to her mother's home in Walthamstow leaving Bethnal Green behind forever.

Chapter Two

In 1919 Jesse was demobbed from the Army and came home for good. During the last few months he had travelled around the country with the Labour Corps, which had given him a chance of a few days leave every so often. Mill had since had another daughter whom they named Vera and with their young family of three girls had now moved from Netley Road to no. 7 Glenthrone Road. Glenthorne Road was at the bottom end of the High Street and close to the junction between St. James's Street, Coppermill Lane and Blackhorse Road. It was the next turning on the left after Hazelwood Road. With the war now over, Mr McLeod had put the Netley Road house up for sale as he said would be his plan when Mill had rented it four years earlier. They had no choice now but to move on although she and Jesse had been very grateful to have rented the house for as long as they had.

Now back home for good he knew he would have to set about finding work. Thousands had come back to nothing, absolutely nothing. Many did get a pension for their disabilities but that would only be for six months or so and then they were left to fend for themselves. There was no work, no financial help, no counselling and certainly no acknowledgement from the government or any help for these heroic men. Gone were the politician's promises of returning to a land fit for heroes. Many were now reduced to begging on the streets or busking in hope that some kind person would take pity and throw a few pence their way. Men who had been blinded in explosions were often seen being led by another wounded soldier; numerous men with limbs missing were begging on the streets just to survive. Some selling matches and shoe laces, anything to put a morsel of food into the mouths of their children. Families were living in poverty and for many the dreaded Workhouse was now the only option they had. Brave men who had fought for their country were separated from their wives and children with no hope for the future once they were admitted into these institutions. Yes, Britain had won the war and Germany had been defeated. It had been a victory for the King and the country but it had been paid for with millions of lives lost and the hero's who did came back were left destitute.

Jesse was truly thankful that he had a decent home to come back to, often he wondered how he had survived it all and found it hard to believe that he really was back in England. He knew he was one of the fortunate ones and he would never ever forgot those he had seen lying dead in the battlefields of France and Belgium, memories that would continue to disturb him until his dying day.

His trade before he had joined up in 1915 was French Polishing and although times were now hard and there wasn't a lot of money to spare he did manage to find some occasion work and Mill helped out by taking in machine work for a local factory. There was also the Army pension of 11/- per week that he had been awarded through his medical condition. He had often inhaled chlorine gas fumes from the soldier's bodies and clothing while he and Father Scholfield, the priest who Jesse had served with, attended the unfortunate men who had been very badly affected or lay dying. He was still suffering from stress and had heart and chest problems which were the reason for him being hospitalised in Manchester for several weeks after being sent home from France, but he was thankfully improving and the pension was for only 26 weeks.

Like thousands of others, Jesse came home from the war a changed man. He had seen so many terribly heart wrenching sights of death and mutilation and the horror of it haunted him in the nightmares that plagued him during the hours of darkness. He was quick to lose his temper and often sat crying when he thought no one was about. His thoughts were often of Frank, the young lad who had been with him in those shell holes. He wished he'd known what happened to him, did he survive? Had he make it back home? He prayed that he hadn't been killed but he would never know. Mill was very patient and understanding but sometimes they often ended up having the most violent arguments. He would go into rage if ever he saw Mill throw a few crusts of bread out for the birds, this was understandable as they had both known what the word starvation meant and she soon learnt not to antagonise him and gave in to many disagreements just to keep the peace.

Three years later in 1922 Mill gave birth to their fourth child and after having three daughters a son was born who they named Jesse Thomas. Jesse after his father and Thomas after one of Mill's brothers although the new baby was soon to be known as 'young' Jesse and his father became 'old' Jesse.

Another three years were to pass and then their fifth and last child was born. Jesse was pleased that he had another son and they named him Ronald Ernest. Ernest after another of Mill's brothers and Ronald being a name they both liked, although he was soon known as Ronnie. Life was better for them now being Jesse did get some French Polishing jobs now and again but they were hard to come by and they were just about managing but with five children money was still short.

In 1927 Jesse was very upset to hear the sad news that the Priest who he had served with during those terrible times in France had died.

Jesse had not seen Father Bernard Schofield since he had returned from serving abroad although they had exchanged one or two letters but the kindly Father had since gone to Manchester to become the very first Prior at the Servite Church of Our Lady of Seven Dolours and St Benedict in a place named Kersal. Two years later his health began to suffer and he went on to take over as Prior in the Servite Church at Bognor, no doubt hoping that the fresh sea air would help with his breathing difficulties and ill health. Jesse always kept the very first letter he received from Father Bernard.

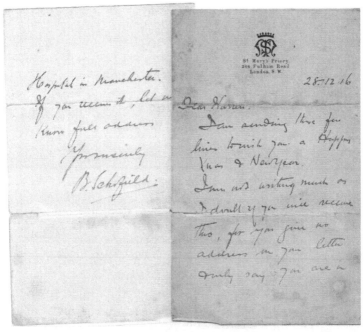

A letter to Jesse from father Bernard from St. Mary's Priory in Fulham Road, London dated 28th December 1916 and sent to Jesse who had just returned from France and was in a Manchester hospital.

The letter reads;
Dear Warren, I am sending these few lines to wish you a happy Xmas and New Year. I am not writing much as I don't know if you will receive this, for you gave no address in your

185

letter only say that you are in a hospital in Manchester. If you receive it let me know your full address, Yours sincerely, B.Scholfield

Sadly Father Bernard Schofield passed away in the September of 1927 from heart failure, cardis vascular degeneration and chronic nephritis he was 44 years old. Illness which could easily be associated with the time he spent in France where he helped so many men who had been gassed. He died in St John & St Elizabeth Hospital London and had come back from Bognor to end his days in his own Parish. Solemn Requiem Mass was celebrated and Father Bernard was interred at St Thomas's Church, Fulham and his obituary appeared in the Catholic newspaper *'The Universe'* Jesse was sad to hear of his passing and hoped that he may Rest in Peace.

Around this time Mill and Jesse had taken in a lodger, Ol'Fatty Whiter as he was known because of his pure white hair and no doubt the fact that he was obese. He wasn't called ol' Fatty out of disrespect and he never found this nick name offensive because it certainly wasn't intended.

He was also known to wear a black bowler hat where ever he went and Mill swore that he even wore it in bed. No one knew his true age but Jesse thought him to be in his seventies and 'getting on a bit'. He was a nice old fellow but he never talked much about his past although they'd heard that his whole family had been wiped out by the Influenza epidemic during the early 1900's. He settled in well with the family and the boys became very fond of him.

With ol' Fatty's encouragement and because of his own rough upbringing and the need of being able to 'look after' himself in times of trouble, Jesse decided to teach his sons to box. He hoped it would toughen them up and get them out of any sticky situations that may arise but there was only one pair of gloves between the two of them so they had to take it in turns sparing with their father. Ronnie and young Jesse were happy to have a turnabout but after one of them gave old Jesse an almighty whack that sent him flying backwards he decided he'd had enough and decided to make them a punch bag which he would hang from the lintel over the back door. He found one of Mill's old bolster cases and stuffed it with rags and old newspapers which the boy's were delighted with. Mill used to often joke that Jesse probably hid his money in there because she never knew where he kept it. It must have paid off because both of the lads went on to win medals for their school boxing, swimming and football teams.

However, it had been ol' Fatty, although getting on in years, who had taught the boys to swim. He also took them to places of interest in London whenever the weather was fine and on one of these outings took them to the Monument. He explained to them that was where the Great fire of London had started in 1666 at a Bakers shop in Pudding Lane.

Of course the boys wanted to climb the 345 steps to the top of the Monument and ol' Fatty being the large man he was had a great struggle getting up there. Then after resting for a while until he got his breath back, he pointed out the many sights of London that could be seen from the top of the 200ft high column. From this advantage point they could see the River Thames with it tugs and barges and ol' Fatty promised to take them to see the ships. It was only after they had returned to the bottom that Fatty suddenly declared, "Sod it! I've left me bowler up there!" None of them wanted to climb all the way back up again so Fatty decided that he'd rather buy a new bowler than make that long climb to the top again. That, he said would be a much better option but often wondered afterwards who was now wearing his old bowler. Then as he had promised, they went to see the ships that were tied up along the Thames Embankment and ol' Fatty got talking to the old sea Captain of a Tramp Steamer. This resulted in letting the boys go on board to have a look around the ship and even stand at the ships wheel on the bridge. It was days like this that Ronnie and young Jesse would remember all their lives but meanwhile they couldn't wait to get home to tell the rest of the family that 'ol' Fatty's left 'is bowler up the Monument and we've been on a boat!"

In the years when money had so often been short Mill, like many other local housewives, would regularly visit Fish Bros. the jeweller in the High Street on the corner of Linden Road which also had a discrete entrance to a Pawn Shop and was always known locally as 'Uncles'. This visit usually took place on a Monday morning when Jesse's best suit went in pawn. Then she would redeem it on the Friday so as he would be able to wear it on Saturday night when he went to the Working Man's club in Buxton Road or for an evening at the local dog track. This was something Jesse never ever knew about, she made sure of that.

If he had known his best suit was more often in pawn than out he would have gone berserk but it would never have occurred to him that Mill needed more money especially with five children to feed and rent to pay let alone money for coal and other household expenses. Although with the three girls now working and contributing that was a big help.

Also in Linden Road, a short turning leading into Selbourne Road where the brick fields had once been was Annie's the second hand clothes shop. She always boasted of having 'good quality stuff from up West' even though it would be piled in heaps on the shop floor and women would sort through it always finding something that would fit someone in their family and the prices were reasonable too.

The war had changed old Jesse and even after all they suffered at the start of it he, like many other men, gave what they thought would 'do' for housekeeping and that was that. The rest, what little there was, was his. To ask for more money would cause even more rows and Mill knew that since his terrible experiences Jesse, although he loved her and his children dearly, had a vile temper which could be aroused very quickly and he had been known to get violent. So again, to keep the peace, she managed the best she could because he was the man of the house and she never asked for extra money in fear of causing another argument.

In 1933 he had a stroke of good luck when he heard of work going at Wrighton's a furniture makers who had just built a large factory at the Crooked Billet on the boarders of Walthamstow and Chingford. He applied for the job and to his relief was taken on. It was here that he learnt the trade of cabinet making.

However, with him now being in a full time employment at Wrighton's things were better but she still had to watch the pennies and still occasionally made the trip to the pawn shop, no doubt to cover the odd bet when she fancied a bet on the dogs or horses.

Saturday night became the highlight of the week for old Jesse. He would go to the local Buxton Club for a few pints with his mates and sometimes Mill went along too or occasionally they would both go to the Walthamstow Dog Track on the Chingford Road for a flutter. Mill's favourite bet was on numbers 6 and 1 which she did 'each way'. Having a Saturday night out now and again was a treat for her too but if she lost at the dogs Jesse's suit would certainly be back in the pawn shop again on the following Monday morning.

1936 proved to be a very eventful year, apart from King George V dying and the scandal of Edward VIII and Mrs Simpson, other events took place in the family.

Firstly in the May, Mill's father Joseph paid a visit to her in Glenthorne Road as he always did on a Saturday morning, he sat down in his usual chair by the fireplace, looked at Mill his eldest child and said, 'I've had a good innings' and promptly

189

died. Not only was it a terrible shock for her but also it really upset Sarah her mother who had hoped for some reason that when his time came he would die at home.

It was said that four of Sarah's sons carried their deceased father back to Cranbrook Road so it could be recorded that he had passed away there and not at Mill's. However, his death certificate does state that he did indeed die at Glenthorne Road but he was certainly taken back to Sarah at some time where he was laid out in the front parlour. His coffin was draped with a Union Jack and his War medals placed along the top. He was given one of the grandest funerals that Walthamstow had ever seen and an account of it was in the local newspaper.

When he was carried from the house his coffin was placed on an open carriage that was decked in flowers and pulled by 2 magnificent black horses with purple plumes. That day Cranbrook Road was filled with neighbours watching the proceedings while more carriages awaited the family. Members of the local British Legion were in attendance as were the Directors of Malcolm Macleod's whom he'd worked for, apart from the war years, since first coming to Walthamstow many years earlier.

One by one they left the house, led by Sarah wearing full mourning clothes followed by their children, all dressed in black. The women wore veils over their faces and the men wore black ties and armbands as they emerged from the house in order of ages. They in turn were followed by various other family members and friends.

Joseph was taken to his last resting place at Queen's Road Cemetery where rows of daffodils in pots lined the path from the main gates to the grave where he was to be buried.

The newspaper reports state that he was held in high esteem and enjoyed much popularity.

It also states that owing to his sudden death, the wedding of his daughter Elsie who was due to marry on the Whitson

Saturday had to be postponed. Elsie did marry at a later date to an Alfred Cullum and they only ever had the one child.

Sarah lived on for another 17 years and when she died in 1953 aged 86 she was laid to rest with her husband Joseph. Since Joseph's death seventeen years earlier, the grave had been attended to every single day throughout the year regardless of the weather by at least one of their sons or daughters who always bought fresh flowers. Sometimes they accompanied each other but not one day would be missed until the death of the last remaining son Harold who died in 1998 aged 87.

Ernest one of their boys also married in the year of 1936 as did young Milly, Mill & Jesse's eldest daughter. She wed John (Jack) Proudfoot in the July. The other event was that King Edward V111 abdicated and George V1 became King. A street party was arranged to celebrate his Coronation and a good old East End '*knees up*' was had by all. Mill had made herself a pair of red, white and blue bloomers with white bobbles and bells around the hem of the legs. (It was believed that she had made these years ago when a party was held for celebrating the end of W.W.1)

She kept those bloomers for many years and always wore them for any celebration party that went on in the street or one of the nearby houses. 1936 was certainly a year many people would not forget in a hurry.

And so life carried on for Mill and old Jesse, although they had kept in touch with Jesse's aunt Amy for many years, she had since passed away and so had his father who had died in 1930 from throat cancer. Jesse had heard from an old East End mate that the old man had remarried years back but he never had much to do with him although Jesse did see his sister Annie from time to time.

Annie and Jesse were the only two children who had survived from several others their mother had given birth to

Milly (Elizabeth) Warren and Jack (John) Proudfoot's Wedding July 25th 1936

St Michaels's Church, Palmeston Road, Walthamstow.

Mill's two sisters' were bridesmaids: Cissy (Beatrice) to Milly's right and Vera left.

before her early death when she was only 27 years old. Annie had married an Arthur Fulshaw and had four children but sadly Arthur her husband had died when he was only 35 years old, Annie herself passed away in her 40's.

By 1939 Britain was again at war with Germany. Mill knew old Jesse would not be called up as he was now getting on for 46 but she knew with fear in her heart that her two sons young Jesse and Ronnie might be. She prayed that it wouldn't come to that but of course in time it did and both boys joined the Navy, first Jesse being the elder and later Ronnie when he got his calling up papers. Jesse had gone along to the Royal Naval recruiting offices in Romford in 1940 to volunteer with Freddie Bailey a mate he'd known for years. He knew he and Freddie would no doubt be called up at some time and they both decided that if they did have to go then they both wanted to serve in the Royal Navy. If they waited to be called up then they might have to join the Army or the Air Force so as he and his mate saw it, this was the best way of making sure they got in.

Young Jesse decided it would be better not to tell his mother but to wait and see what transpired because he knew how she would react.

It was a few days before Christmas and almost two years later when he came home from work one evening to find his mother very upset and agitated as she pointed to a long buff envelope propped against the mantelpiece clock. Along the top were the words,

'*On His Majesty's Service*'. "You silly bugger!" she cried, "You've bloody well been an' signed on!" Little did she know he had done it two years earlier.

Young Jesse opened the envelope and found he had been accepted and was to be; O/Seaman Warren and had to report to H.M.S. Glendower a Naval depot in Wales to begin his training in February.

Mill was very distraught,

"Wait 'til yer ol' man finds out, he'll go potty" she cried. And he did. However what was done was done, they couldn't change anything. Old Jesse tried to console Mill by saying it wouldn't be like the last lot; this would be a different sort of war. Even so, many men would die, it was inevitable but he prayed as Mill did that their boys wouldn't be taken if the worst came to the worst.

Young Jesse had been working for Austin's a cabinet making factory in Lea Bridge Road in nearby Leyton and the day before Christmas Eve he was called in to see the foreman. He knew what this was about and had been expecting it, he was going to be laid off which happened every Christmas. To save having to pay their workers for holiday time they were all sacked and then reinstated in the New Year. The men were very annoyed and distraught about this because to lose pay at this time of year caused hardships for many and there was a lot of talk about joining a workers union but so far it hadn't happened. So when young Jesse got the message to go into the foreman's office he was prepared because in his white carpenters apron pocket was the letter he'd received a couple of days before.

The office was really just a small part of the shop floor that had been petitioned off but it made the foreman feel more important and gave him an air of authority. He was sitting behind a small wooden table on a fold up camping chair wearing his long brown 'official' coat.

"Sorry Warren but I'm afraid the management have asked me to tell yer that we've got to let yer go"

"Oh, yeah is that right then?"

"Well, yes but yer job will be open for yer if you want to come back after Christmas."

Young Jesse had been waiting for this, "Well you can go and tell the management" he said, emphasising the word *'management,'* that they can stick their job right up their arse!"

The foreman suddenly stood up knocking over the flimsy chair and banging clenched fists on the table leant towards Jesse.

"Now just you look 'ere, yer can't talk to me like that!"

"Can't I? Well, if yer don't like it then hard luck"

"If yer taking that attitude then don't bother coming back after Christmas" he replied bending down to retrieve the chair and promptly sat down again, "someone will soon take yer place so don't come crawling back 'ere when yer can't get another job"

"I've already got one" Jesse replied as he took the brown envelope from his pocket and waved it towards the foreman, "I've joined the Navy"

The foreman looked a bit aghast, "Christ mate how old are yer?"

"I'm nineteen and I'll have yer know I signed on a couple of years back but they've only just called me up and to tell yer the truth I'll be glad to get out of this bloody dump!"

The foreman stared at him for a moment then stood up and walked around the table towards him and held out his hand. Jesse hesitated for a few seconds and took it as the foreman said, "I didn't know mate" and shaking his hand added, "Good luck son and I wish yer all the best".

As Jesse left the small office the foreman lent his elbows on the table and rested his head in his hands as memories of his own time serving in the navy during the last war came back to him… 'God help him' he thought, 'God help them all'.

By now young Milly had given birth to a son and named him John after his father. Sadly he died at 10 weeks old but David their second child who was born in 1938 was thriving and when he was three years old in 1941 John (Jack) his father, had been called up and was now in the Army. The following year in the November of 1942 I myself was born and became Mill and Jack's third child.

The war was raging on and thankfully Glenthorne Road had been spared of having any direct hits although some unfortunate people living in Hazlewood Road, the next turning had received the first fatality of the war. Anderson shelters had been erected in most back gardens including no.7 and also further along the road where young Milly and her family were now living. David, my brother still remembers being in one of these shelters while the bombing was going on over Walthamstow and recalls our Aunt Cissy reading him stories during those terrible times. I myself have hardly any memories of those days except the when someone shouting excitedly, 'Look, look, there's a doddle- bug!' These flying V1 bombs, (official name 'Pilotless Aircraft') or 'doodle-bugs' as they were soon called by the British public, were first seen over London in the June of 1944. I would have only been 19 months old at the time so it must have been some time later when this one was spotted over Walthamstow. I pride myself in having a good memory but I don't think it's that good! However, I do have a slight memory of being taken to Trafalgar Square with David to feed the pigeons.

My sister Irene Veronica was born in 1945 but sadly on the Christmas Eve of that year she also died at just 10 months old from Bronchitis. Nowadays antibiotics would have saved her but in those days they just weren't available and the only thing they could use in hope of the child surviving was a hot poultice. This consisted of a sheet of brown paper smeared with hot wet bread and placed on the patient's chest at a bearable heat. A knob of butter was given to the child so that it would grease the chest from within as it melted in the mouth.

Above Jesse Warren (far left) at Wrighton's c.1935

Below Ronnie (left) and Young Jesse (right)

197

Hot milk with butter floating on the top was also a remedy and apart from keeping the child warm little else could be done. To lose a child at any time is a most dreadful thing and one cannot even imagine the pain and anguish that Milly and Jack and indeed the whole family suffered that Christmas. Losing John their firstborn child was tragic enough and then to lose another baby, that was so sad. John died from what was known as a twisted gut, again something that have could have been remedied by a operation but it appears that this operation wasn't available during this time. John was buried at Queen's Road cemetery in front of a long wall which was allocated for very young babies. Irene was laid to rest in a family plot belonging to the Herod's also in Queen's Road.

Jack was given compassionate leave when Irene died and in his grief went to his mother's house in Hamilton Road, Walthamstow and sat at her piano and played continuously throughout the night. No one bothered him and left him to deal with this terrible loss in his own way.

Situated behind the gardens of the houses on the right hand side of Glenthorne Road was the creosote manufacture or factory as it was known locally. Premises like this would never be permitted nowadays because of the fire hazards of this highly inflammable and no doubt toxic substance. No one thought of the dangers it held for the people living in the nearby houses and in those days there was no such thing as Health & Safety rules. As it was this factory did catch fire late one Sunday night and caused a great deal of excitement as all the residents leant from their back bedroom windows to watch as the flames lit up the sky. It was only when the smell and choking fumes nearly overpowered them all that they came in and slammed their windows shut. Although the fire brigade was soon on hand it burnt on for several days much to the annoyance of the housewives who couldn't hang out their Monday washing but it was a great delight for all the local kids who though it was 'smashing!' The smell lingered on for weeks and I very much doubt if the factory ever opened up again.

Meantime, Ol' Fatty had got the notion to dye his pure white hair black but it went wrong and as a result it ended up a bright orange colour much to everyone's amusement. When asked why he'd done it he rather sheepishly explained that he'd wanted to look younger to find a job and get back into work but unfortunately having hair the colour of oranges soon put paid to that idea. As Mill suggested, it would be best to just let it grow out and wait until his natural colour grew back and to forget about getting a job.

He always got on well with the family and like with this incident, there was never a dull moment with him living in the house, especially when he devised his own 'Air Raid Evacuation Plan' which caused even more amusement. Worried about getting out of the house or at least out of *his* room should a fire break out or the air raid siren started warning them of an impending bombing attack, he decided he needed a way to get out of the house quickly and down into the shelter. So he came up with an escape plan. He found a long sturdy length of rope which he tied around the foot of his heavy old brass bed and let the rope hang from the bedroom with the sash window closed just above it.

One morning hearing an almighty crash, Mill ran upstairs to see what had caused it. Lying flat on the floor in his flannel combinations and mumbling several unrepeatable oaths was ol' Fatty who had forgotten about his escape route and had fallen arse over 'ead (as Mill told everyone later) over the rope that was stretched across the room.

Marion and David feeding the pigeons. Auntie Cissy is on the left and Auntie Vera on the right. No doubt my mother Milly was taking the photo. C.1945

Mill struggled to help him up but thankfully the rope was never needed because of an air raid or a fire but it certainly did come in handy one day when he was out of the window and down that rope as fast as you could say 'Jack Flash!" Even at his age he certainly proved to be pretty nimble on this occasion. He'd gone to put on his boots and found a family of mice had nested in one of them. His fear of mice and rats was well known and he was terrified of them, so much so that he quickly pulled up the slash window climbed over the window sill and made a hasty exit down the rope and into the garden below. It was Mill who removed the mice by tipping them into a cardboard box but not before one had run up her arm, jumped off her shoulder and then ran under the bed. It took some persuading for Fatty to return to his room and eventually he did so after being reassured that the mice had left. Although Mill never let on to ol'Fatty that one had gone under his bed and hadn't come out!

Mill with granddaughter Marion. c.1946

Marion with brother David VE Day

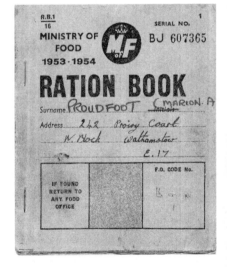

Chapter Three

After the war ended in May 1945, Mill and old Jesse decided to start up their own business. He had learnt the trade of cabinet making while at Wrighton's and was already a skilled French Polisher with years of experience.

Young Jesse had been medically discharged from the Navy after serving for two years. While on parade at Chatham Docks he found it difficult to hold his rifle or to salute his commanding officer. This caused a lot of problems and he was charged with disobedience but eventually it was accepted that he had a medical condition. He had many tests done in Naval hospitals and was eventually diagnosed with a very rare and terribly crippling disease, Siringomyelocle which only effects one in every 100,000 people. Although it was always said and thought that it was caused by a 'germ' which he contracted while at Chatham Docks the real cause at the time was never known and he was discharged with a pension. However, it is now known that Siringomyelocle is a form of spina bifida caused by a sac of fluid at the base of the spine.

Although young Jesse was having difficulties with his hands he could still manage working with carpentry tools and he'd learnt the trade while at Austin's before he'd signed up so this venture would be run as a family business. Suitable premises were found in Markhouse Road which adjoined St. James Street, again not far from the Walthamstow High Street. Old Jesse had given it a lot of thought and had come up with the idea of opening a Cabinet makers, French Polishing and Upholstery shop.

Both the boys, Ronnie learning from his father and elder brother, had woodworking skills and Mill had proved to be an excellent machinist and always boasted that she could make anything from a baby's dress to a pair of curtains or a cushion cover to upholstering a complete three piece suite for indeed she could. She had been machining ever since those early days before they had even married many years back, so she really could turn her hand to anything and very often did.

They also thought that having their own business would be work for the boys and although young Jesse was no longer in the services it would be something for Ron to have when he returned, not like the 1914-18 War when thousands of men had come home to nothing.

So after having lived at 7, Glenthorne Road since 1919, they packed up home and moved to 105 Markhouse Road which they rented from their new neighbours, Ester and Rubin Cohen who had the clothes shop next door at 103.

It was sad leaving all their old friends and neighbours that they had got to know during the years they lived in Glenthorne Road but they felt it was the right time to move on. They had shared some good times together and those terrible years as war raged over Walthamstow. Those were the times they would always remember and would never forget their old friends and neighbours.

They wouldn't never forget 'Streaky' Green so called because he was described as a 'long tall streak of nothing' and was always running; 'Chicky Chick' so called because her father sold chickens and eggs in the Walthamstow market but no one ever knew her real name and even her parents were known as Mr & Mrs. Chick. They lived on the corner of the ally-way leading to the creosote factory behind the houses. There was Elsie Bucket, so called because her real name was Elsie Powell (Pail). Then there were the Hurran's; Mrs Hurran was a money leader and Mill had got to know her very well indeed, for obvious reasons.

She had three sons, Fred, Sonny and Ben who played football for a team called 'The Glens'. Jesse Snr, young Jesse and

Ronnie would often go to watch ·them play on Sunday mornings on the Marshes not far from where they lived.

There was also a park keeper that lived in Glenthorne Road but the kids all steered clear of him because he shouted at them and told them to 'bugger off' whenever they played outside his house, he also had a son. This son was nicknamed 'Soapy' on account that he never washed and all the mothers in the road agreed that he could do with a good 'soaping'. And then there was Sarah. Now, Sarah wasn't really a woman at all but a bloke by the name of Newman. He or she, would wear a man's suit with a trilby hat worn at an angle on the side of his head and painted his nails. He wore bright red lipstick and powdered and painted his face with rouge and added thick black eyebrows. He liked nothing better than sitting in his upstairs bedroom window posing, much to the amusement and micky taking of the local children. Sarah had been called up and joined the Royal Navy when World War Two had broken out. However, one evening while in the Long Bar at Chatham Dockyard he/she was beaten up by several sailors, so severely that after a long stay in hospital he was invalided out of the Navy. He did recovered but was never able to work again although he became a really good piano player, always in demand at parties and by playing in the local pubs he earned a living. It was never known to what extent his injuries had been but the unfortunate man must have suffered very badly.

Next door to no.7 lived the Sidney's who the Warren's did not get along with at all. The Warren's thought them to be a bit too 'posh' for the street because not only did they have a conservatory on the back of their house, they kept their biscuits in a real biscuit barrel and not an old tin as Mill did. Apparently according to young Jesse who had by chance been invited in next door on one occasion, said it was so filthy in there that he felt like taking his shoes off when he came out, not like most places where you take them off when you go in!

It was Mr. Sidney who got young Ronnie into trouble one day. He didn't like Mill so gave Ronnie a sixpence and told him to go back home and shout, "Sod off!" to his mum.

Ronnie did as he was bid and in return got a clip around the ear and promptly ran upstairs crying. Whenever Ronnie was in trouble or had got a telling off they always knew where to find him...............under his bed! So that's where he'd rushed off to, his own special retreat although he was only doing what Mr Sidney had told him.

Apart from other friends and neighbours there was Emily and Bert Simmons who's son Walter married Mill and Jesse's youngest daughter Vera. In those days no one would have believed that Em (as she was known) and Bert would later become the Mayor and Mayoress of Walthamstow. There was also the Kelly family who suffered a terrible tragedy when one of the daughters was running along the road with a pair of scissors in her hand. She had been asked to return them to a neighbour from whom they had been loaned. Unfortunately she tripped and fell and the scissors penetrated one of her eyes and she not only lost her sight but also the eye.

It was also here in Glenthorne Road and many other roads in the area that the 'tally man' would call selling all manner of house hold goods and items that could be paid for on a weekly basis. The method of purchasing these items became known as the getting them on the 'never, never' or 'the knock-knock,' so called because many housewives never seemed to be out of debt and more than often when the tally-man did 'knock' they pretended to be out. Numerous things such as sheets and bedding would soon be in the pawn shop and if a husband happened to answer the tally man's knock there'd be many who had no idea who this bloke, asking for money was and would most likely tell him to bugger off.

However, 'Uncle's' the local Pawn Shop knew only too well…so no, Mill and Jesse would without doubt never forget those friends and neighbours from Genthrone Road.

Thankfully Ronnie returned home safely from the Second World War. The whole family had survived not only the Blitz over London but also the terrible times, fears and uncertainties that any wars bring. Mercifully not one of the Proudfoot's, Herod's or the Warren's had been lost.

When Ronnie who had served on the B.Y.M.S. Minesweepers out in Hong Kong and Rangoon (Burma) returned home it was to find that,

J. F. Warren & Sons
Cabinet Makers, Upholsters & French Polishers

were now open for business at 105 Markhouse Road. The whole shop front was decked out with red, white and blue bunting to welcome him back and a big sign hung across the shop windows which read;

'Welcome Home Ronnie'

This was now his new home being the family had moved whilst he was overseas but he didn't care where they'd moved to be ….he was so thankful that he had made it back safely and all his family had survived the bombings and the Blitz. He had lost some close mates during the war and had known several ratings that had sadly gone down on H.M.S. HOOD. All the Warren's were devastated to hear this heart-rendering news not only because of the terrible tragedy that it was but because several of the young men who died had been to a party at Markhouse Road only several months before.

Young men who'd had so much to live for; it was indeed a very sad and tragic loss.

Jesse and Mill knew how very fortunate they were that their sons (my two uncles) had been spared and were home safely, even though by now young Jesse had an illness for which there was no known cure and would gradually worsen as the years passed.

They all knew and had heard of so many who had lost their lives during those terrible years and Mill prayed that none of them who had survived would ever have to go through it ever again. So many, like those who had served in the First War hadn't *given* their lives for their country for as young Jesse would often say with bitterness and resentment, 'They had them snatched away from them' Thousands would never return to their homes nor to their loved ones who were left behind to grieve at their loss. They had been young men with so much to live for but now they were gone. Mill closed her eyes and whispered, 'May they all rest in peace and may they never ever be forgotten'.

Number 105 Markhouse Road was a very large glass fronted shop with the entrance door being on the far right set back in a porch facing the road. Glass display cabinets that were made on the premises, along with occasional tables were placed to their best advantage in the window along with any newly reupholstered chairs and other items that were awaiting collection from customers. This was a way of advertising the quality of their work, which indeed was very good and so the business venture began to take off.

When armchairs or couches were brought in to be repaired or completely reupholstered I was given the job of searching the backs for any items that may have been lost by the customer over the years. Old Jesse would cut open the old shabby covering with a sharp knife just above the lower wooden frame and I would eagerly see what I could find; knitting needles, scissors, loose change of little value, sweet papers, cigarette packets, an occasional post card or letter but never anything of value like jewellery or diamond rings.

There were two doors at the rear of the shop, one leading to a back room where old Jesse did his French Polishing and another leading down a long passage way to a small sitting room and a scullery (although it became known as a kitchen) which led to a medium sized garden. The only lavatory in the property was outside by the back door.

When old Jesse, suitably attired in his white apron, was either polishing a newly made item or re-polishing an old piece for a customer the strong smell of cellulose would drift throughout the rooms. To prevent any dust rising from the stone floor he would fill a watering can and sprinkle the floor with water before starting on his next project. Sometimes he would let me sprinkle the water which I thought was great fun. There was an occasion when he was overcome by the fumes of the cellulose and no doubt the white spirits that he also used. I once overheard, when my grandmother was telling someone about it, that his throat had been on fire. Being just a young child I had imagined real flames coming from his mouth!

At the bottom of the garden and built against a high wooden fence that backed onto an ally way, stood a very large shed which took up the whole width of the garden. This was ideal for storing the various cuts of wood needed for making cabinets and occasional commissioned pieces. Sheets of very thin veneer of various shades and markings were laid flat in a pile beside an assortment of timber in all widths and lengths. It also contained a large table saw and a big vice that was attached to a wooden benches. Sawdust and wood shavings like big wooden curls often covered the floor giving off a wonderful smell of cedar, pine and oak. A door at the back of the shed opened into the ally way that led from Ringwood

Road on the left and along to a factory towards the right. At five minutes to one the factories loud hooter sounded summoning the workers after their lunch break and then on the dot a 1 o'clock it went again. No one could use excuses like their watch or clock had stopped for being late for work.

The garden had the remains of an air raid shelter that served as a coal shed and opposite that a small chicken coop where Mill kept a dozen or so chickens.

There was no bathroom in the house but they did have a large long tin bath hanging from the wall around the side of the house which would be dragged into the kitchen every Friday night.

A massive mangle with very heavy wooden rollers and an enormous iron wheel with many cogs and a protruding handle that was used to wring water from the clothes was kept in the kitchen. Underneath to catch the water, sat a very large white enamel bowl with a blue rim. To heat any water needed for the weekly wash or bathing there was an old gas boiler that always seemed to be giving off fumes. No doubt due to the crude rubber piping that had been connected from the boiler to a gas pipe near the gas stove.

There was also a small walk in pantry to the right of the back door which had shelves and a large stone slab for storing fresh food stuff and in the wall at the back, a small window for ventilation. A shallow brown sink with a ribbed design along the front was to the left of the back door. There was a high narrow window that not only looked out onto a concreted area which ran alongside the house but over a low fence into the Cohen's who's house and garden was next door.

Also on the outside wall hang another small bath which Mill used for the weekly washing and under the kitchen sink she kept a glass scrubbing board, scrubbing brushes and blocks of green soap. There also stood a large wooden table and an old grey gas cooker on legs. Mill was really pleased that the house had a gas cooker because she'd only had the old black leaded kitchen range to use when they were in Glenthorne Road.

Back along the passage way and opposite the door that opened into the shop, were the stairs that led up to a small landing, to the right was a bedroom with a smaller room at the rear where a window looked out over the back garden and work shed. To the left of the landing a short flight of stairs led to a more spacious area that would serve as a bar whenever one of their frequent parties was going on. Empty wooden beer creates piled two high would support a sturdy length of wood and next to that at one end rested a hefty barrel of ale on trestles.

Opposite this was a bedroom with a big fireplace. From the long sash window to the right, one could look down to the side of the house being this room was above the room below where old Jesse did his polishing and where French doors lead out to the side of the house and the garden. Once, when a party was in full swing, there must have been quite a queue for the outside lavatory because I happened to have looked out when I was supposed to be in bed asleep and there standing against the wall of the house several men were all lined up relieving themselves! I never ever told a soul as to what I'd seen.

The next door on the landing to the right of the bedroom led to the room above the shop. This was a very spacious room indeed being the same size as the shop below which must have been at least 30' in length and quite wide too. It had three long sash windows that overlooked the road outside and the shops opposite. At the far end of the room was a fire place with a tiled surround

Markhouse Road itself was a very busy road with heavy traffic trundling past and it was also a bus route for Leyton and Leytonstone or in the opposite direction, Chingford.

The shop next door to the left, number 107, sold Scott motor cycles but living in a couple of rooms at the back was an illegal book maker.

Mill and old Jesse were delighted when they discovered the book maker living there was some guy who had dealings at the local dog tracks because they both liked a flutter on the dogs and after a while they had a wind up telephone fitted up which connected them directly to 107. They were then able to place their bets without anyone seeing them having to go into next door.

In those days it was illegal to be a unlicensed book maker and many 'bookies runners' were fined for collecting bets illegally on behalf of these book-makers (my own father had at one time been a bookies runner and he always boasted that he'd never got caught)

Further along the road to the left was Trotter's the radio shop where as a child I had to take an accumulator to be recharged as this served as a battery for the wireless. An accumulator was a square glass jar filled with lead acid and there were screws at the top so it could be refilled (or charged up) at a cost of 3d (approx. 2.5p)

Who would nowadays allow a child to walk along the road with something so dangerous? If I had fallen or tripped and it had smashed then goodness knows what horrifying injuries I could have received from the acid. Thankfully it didn't happen.

Then there was a lamp shade shop, a café and 'Kitty's' the cat's meat shop. The woman who ran the shop was called Kitty and had that name above the shop front which was rather apt considering she sold meat for cats. The meat she sold was unfit for human consumption or so the sign in her window said although many a man enjoyed a meat pie for his dinner without ever knowing that the filling had come from a cat's meat shop! I know my aunt Elsie, one of my dad's sisters often bought her husband a nice piece of steak from there. 'Well,' she would say, 'it looked alright and smelt alright so why give it to the cat?' Maybe he was just lucky and like the other men who unknowingly enjoyed Kitty's meat, never seemed to come to any harm.

Next shop along was the Barber who had a long red and white pole outside that turned around and reminded me of a stick of rock. These poles went back to the Middle Ages when barbers not only shaved men and cut their hair but were also known for bloodletting, a cure for all ailments and they extracted teeth. The red and white pole was in a way an advertising sign which represented blood and bandages.

Then there was the Laundry which was always known as the bag wash shop. You could take your washing along in a large hessian sack, (usually on an old pram or cart of some sort) and the following day go along to collect it after it had been beautifully washed, spun out and ready to hang on the line. You were given your own personal number which was then marked on any new sack with indelible ink and a ticket with the same corresponding number written on it which served as a receipt for when you collected your clean washing. I remember one day going there with my grandmother to collect her washing when she was accidently given the wrong sack and without noticing the mistake, wheeled it home on an old pushchair specially kept for that purpose. The washing was still sitting untied on the pushchair when a woman came banging on the shop door of 105 which was now locked, in a most terrible rage.

"Oy you!" she shouted through the letter box, "Open up this bloody door 'cos I know you've pinched me bleeding washing!"

Old Jesse unlocked the door with Mill following behind wondering what on earth was going on.

"We ain't got your washing you daft ol' bat" she shouted back to this irate woman who she recognised as living in one of the houses just around the corner in Ringwood Road, "and besides seeing what you 'ang on the line we wouldn't bloody well want it!"

"Ere look!" that's my number on that sack, "they said yer 'ad it so give it back or I'll call the coppers"

Mill agreed it was the wrong sack but the woman still kept ranting and raving insisting she was trying to pinch it.

'Blimey, I wash me floor and clean the lav out with better rags than you've got in there!' Mill retaliated.

Meanwhile, whilst the two women were going hammer and tongs and the woman again threatened to get the police, old Jesse picked the washing up from the pushchair and shouted, "Yeah, you do that, get the bleeding coppers and take yer bloody washing with yer while yer about it!"

With that he threw the sack through the open shop doorway but as it landed the string tying the top up came undone and half the washing fell out onto the pavement.

"Now bugger off and don't come accusing my old lady of pinching yer bloody stuff" He was about to put the bolt on the door when he opened it up again and as an afterthought, called out, "And don't leave any of yer smelly ol' drawers outside my shop!"

"My drawers ain't smelly any more, they've just come from the bag wash!"

I was soon joining in with my grandparents as they fell about laughing.

Later that afternoon old Jesse went down to the bag wash shop to collect the right sack himself and told them to 'sort themselves out' as he put it. This turned out to be a good move on his part because the following week they got a free wash as a way of apology.

Alongside the laundry was the butcher's where I would love to drag my feet through the thick sawdust that was put down daily. This no doubt was to soak up any blood that may run from the fresh meat. Often I was sent to get 'a yard of pork' and the butcher would wrap three pig's trotters in white paper for me to take back to 105. Ask anyone nowadays what a yard of pork was and it's very unlikely they would know. However, in the days before we went over to metric measurements we only used feet, inches and yards. Therefore, being there were three feet to a yard, three pig's feet became a 'yard of pork', which incidentally made a very nourishing meal when boiled with a pound or two of pot-herbs. Pot-'erbs (as they were commonly known), consisted of onions, swedes, carrots and turnips.

Then on the corner of Queen's Road and Markhouse Road was The Common Gate public house (this was said to be a pub where the notorious Kray twins visited when they were in Walthamstow) and on the opposite corner a Post Office. Across the road was the Light House Church, so called because instead of a steeple it had what appeared to be a lighthouse. It was said that the money to build the church was donated by a sea captain and he thought more people would be encouraged to attend church if they saw a revolving light rather than hearing church bells. There was also a chemist, a cobbler's, a fish and chip shop and drapers which sold all manner of haberdashery.

The Cohen's who had a dress shop next door to the Warrens were also their landlords. The clothes sold there were rather classy and said to have come from a manufacturer in the West End and were rather expensive.

Neither Mill nor her daughters ever brought their clothes from there; they went to Lil Woods who sold stuff from her living room in Queen's Road just around the corner. Besides they could pay off a bit each week and Lil marked it down in a book but they wouldn't get the goods until they were paid for in full. Lil Woods was too cute for that.

Davis Dairy was on the corner of Ringwood Road just to the right passed the Cohen's. Around the side of the Dairy was a door where you could knock 'after hours' and just past that the entrance to the ally way that ran behind the shops. The proprietor of Davis's would always be willing to serve you and most of the customers had their shopping put 'on the slate' until the end of the week but the shop keeper always got his money, usually on a Saturday after the husbands had given their wives their housekeeping money for the week. They all knew that if they didn't pay their bill then there would be no more grub until they did.

It was here in Davis's where every Tuesday morning they cooked delicious knuckles of bacon, smoked or green back which cost half a crown (12½p) and sold them while they were still hot.

In those days before self service shops were to become so popular customers would give the assistant their shopping lists when it was their turn to be served and then wait for their groceries to be put in their wicker shopping baskets or packed into a box. Some items like sugar, tea or dried fruit was scooped from big sacks, weighed out and put into dark blue paper bags with the tops securely folded down.

Looking down towards the Lighthouse Church,
Markhouse Road. St Saviour's Church Spire in distance on

Corner of Ringwood and Markhouse Road.
Showing what was once Jesse Warrens shop (105).

Home deliveries were available but shopping didn't arrive in large vans with the driver wheeling foodstuff to the customer's door as they do today. Home deliveries were made by the errand boy whose bike had a large basket above the front wheel. Just like the one Granville had in the T.V Series, 'Open All Hours.'

Some items were still on ration well into the 1950's so there wasn't a lot of choice as to where you could shop for groceries.

However, there were two Davis Dairies in the area, the other being in Station Road just off St James's Street. Their name was stamped inside most Ration Books in the locality, as it was necessary to register with a shop before you could get your weekly rations. The shop in Station Road had a cellar which again was just like the one at Arkwright's in 'Open All Hours' but this one was in the middle of the shop, not behind the counter. I recall being told by Mill, my Nan, not to go near it in case I fell down the steps!

Mill, like most housewives usually shopped daily but if they did run out of anything they needed quickly then a neighbour would always be willing to lend a cup of sugar or an egg or two. Of course with a shop being close by on the corner and a door at the side for when they were closed, Mill didn't need to borrow from her neighbours.

There would always be a couple of chairs placed near the long counter in Davis's shops so women could take the weight off their feet while their order was being put together. It was also a good meeting place for women to discuss their various medical complaints, moan about their husbands, the rationing, the weather or their kids and exchange any local gossip.

On the opposite corner of Ringwood Road was Watson's the linoleum shop whose window display boasted tall upright rolls of floor covering in various lengths, designs and colours. In those days having fitted carpets was never considered an option. Most people would have a large rug in their front parlour, or a few slip mats between doorways and maybe a homemade rag rug in front of the fire, often in the shape of a half moon.

Almost directly opposite the Warren's shop in Markhouse Road stood Pollards the wallpaper and paint shop where paint would be mixed up. Brown, dark green, cream and red seemed to be the most popular colours and a white wash was available for ceilings. If there were any ready to mix wallpaper pastes available in those days' people wouldn't have bought them because a big bucket of flour and water mixed to a smooth paste did the job just as well. It was only years later that people began to realise that when this flour paste dried out it made not only a never ending food supply but a breeding ground for bugs and was one of the main causes for so many houses being infested.

Once bugs started breeding in a house they got everywhere but worst of all were the bed bugs. It was at night when it was dark that these dreaded creatures came out from cracks and crannies and the old iron bedsteads and flock mattresses were known to be a favourite place for them to hide during the day. No doubt the sayings 'Sleep tight, mind the bugs don't bite' and 'as snug as a bug in a rug' came about. Thankfully wallpaper pastes of today have fungicides in them and flour paste for decorating is now a thing of the past. Like-wise it's very rare to hear of bed bug infestations.

Pollards also stocked turpentine and white spirit which was used for cleaning brushes and thinners for making the paint go further. These products were stored in big brown glazed jars with a piece of rag around the cork to keep it fitted tightly into the neck of the jar. If you needed any of this cleaner then you took your own empty beer or lemonade bottle to the shop where an assistant filled it by using a funnel.

The next shop along was Cruikshank's the cycle shop which had a strong distinctive smell of rubber.

The oil shop (as it was known) was next and sold every household item one could want or imagine, from bundles of firewood and paraffin to candles and moth balls; from nails and tools to watering cans and grass seed. There were bars of green scrubbing soaps and washboards, balls of string, brooms and mouse traps. Buckets, chamber pots and the coal scuttles were tied together and hung from the ceiling. If your enamel saucepan, bucket or bowl developed a hole then you asked for a pot mender. This consisted of two washers with a bolt. A washer was placed either side of the hole and then bolted together to form a seal which was a very efficient way of doing a repair. I really loved that shop and to me as a small child, it was just like an Aladdin's Cave and I still recall to this very day, the smell of the soaps and household items on display there.

Akers the bakers who had coal burning ovens in a room behind their shop in which they baked the most mouth watering crusty loaves of bread were next door. It never seemed to bother any of the customers when the baker's cat was seen more often than not sleeping on a tray of warm freshly baked bread. It bothered the cat more when he got shooed off but he soon nestled down on another tray or even on a sunny day ventured into the shop window and sat amongst the rolls and cakes.

Just imagine the hazard of having these four shops altogether! What with paint, turpentine, paraffin, rubber tyres and coal burning ovens one spark and the whole lot could have been blown sky high, probably taking J.F.Warren & Sons with it not forgetting the families who lived behind or above these premises. Thankfully it never happened, however a very amusing event did take place once involving my grandmother and Pollards. And to this very day it still makes me smile:

It happened one day while old Jesse was away for a couple of days doing a bit of French Polishing for a company in Croydon and had stayed over until the job was completed. Sometimes he would get an extra bit of work like this on recommendation

The manager of Pollards had seen Mill come along from the corner dairy and called across to asked her if she was interested in some surplus paint. It seemed they had a lot of red paint that had been mixed wrong and he couldn't sell it because customers said it was far too bright. Being that nobody wanted it he wondered if she could use a couple of tins, free of charge? Mill was delighted with this and of course accepted the offer. At first she didn't know what she could do with it because it certainly wouldn't do inside the house so after giving it some thought she decided that the dark outside lavatory could do with brightening up. She also thought that Fire Engine Red would have been a good name for this colour and no one could argue that it wouldn't brighten up a lav! So it was that she set to and began.

First she painted the walls then the ceiling and the cistern, the long pipe leading down to the white china pan got a coat of bright red paint as did the wooden boxed in seat. Even the nail that held squares of newspaper was painted. In fact every thing in this small lavatory got painted including the inside of the wooden door and small window frame, the outside of the pan and then last of all the floor because there was no sense in letting a good tin of free paint go to waste. As she was painting the inside of the door she thought she must remind old Jess to fill in the three knot holes because she was fed up with them all peeping through while she was in there and asking how long she would be.

When old Jesse returned home the following night it was dark and as always the first thing he did was to go out 'the back' (as the outside lav was known) taking with him the torch that was always left hanging for that purpose on a nail by the back door.

He'd had a few beers with a mate whom he'd met up with as he'd got off the train at James Street Station and they'd gone into the nearby Coach & Horses for a 'quick half' before coming home. He must have had several quick 'half's' because he was a bit worse for wear or as Mill would put it in her not too lady like manner…pissed! She'd been sitting in a easy chair doing a bit of knitting when he came home and was listening to her favourite crooner Donald Peers singing on the wireless, '*In a shady nook by a babbling brook, that's where I fell in love with you……*'

Jesse hadn't been out the back for more than a couple of minutes when all of a sudden she got the fright of her life as he rushed back into the house with his braces hanging down around his legs, his shirt tail flapping and holding up his loose trousers at the front with one hand while almost screaming, "Quick, quick, get a bucket of water! Get a bucket of water!"

"What's the matter with you, you daft ol' sod" she exclaimed jumping up from her seat wondering what of earth was wrong as her knitting fell to the floor.

"Don't just stand there you silly ol' cow!" he shouted, "Quick, quick, get some water…the bloody shit house is on fire, I could 'ave burnt me bleeding arse!"

Seeing unexpectedly a bright red lavatory by torch light would have been quite an alarming sight and must have looked as if it really was on fire. Mill hadn't even thought to warn him about it but the shock certainly sobered him up!

"You dozy cow" he cried, "I could 'ave 'ad a bloody 'eart attack"

I don't think anyone in the family ever forgot that incident after hearing about it, I know I certainly never have and even now it still amuses me when I think about.

Some years later when betting became legal and their bookie neighbour had since moved on, a disused shop the other side of the Cohen's opened as a Betting shop which delighted Mill. And so that old Jesse didn't get to know just how often she went in there she used the name of 'Rosie' on her betting slips, just in case he got wind of it. This way she could always say she was putting a bet on for a friend or a neighbour should he find out. However, one day after she had been confined to her bed for a couple of days with a bad cold, the manager of the shop felt concerned at not seeing her especially being she was such a regular customer. Besides, she had a few bob coming her way so he guessed something was up as she hadn't collected her winnings. By chance he was standing outside his shop during a quiet moment just as Jesse was about to go indoors

"How's Rosie mate" he called out, "Haven't seen her for a couple of days, she alright?"

Jesse turned and looked at him, "Who the bleeding 'ell is Rosie?" he asked in a gruff manner.

"Your other half, that woman I see you with sometimes" replied the man with a friendly smile. Before he knew it Jesse had grabbed him by the collar and shouted into the startled man's face, " 'Ere what yer on about, you trying to be funny 'cos I ain't bleeding carrying on with any Rosie so just you keep yer bloody mouth shut or I'll bleeding land you one" He held his fist to the managers face menacingly. Even though this chap was several inches taller it didn't bother Jesse and he would have smacked him one but it was only the threat of being banned from the Bookies shop that stopped him.

[In 1960 all these shops in Markhouse Road including 105 were condemned by the local Council but as I write in January 2014, many are still standing including the Warren's old shop].

However, there was one shop along Markhouse Road that was my absolute favourite and that was Strutt's the candy shop. It was here that they made the most mouth watering confectionary that anyone who has a sweet tooth could ever imagine and in all my years I have never ever found another shop that can make confectionary like Strutt's did. They had the most wonderful slabs of pink and white or brown and white coconut ice and big balls of white fondant candy with large flakes of coconut inside that was sliced with a knife. I can still recall the wonderful sweet aroma as I walked into that shop with my pocket money and more often than not, eating this delightful treat before I had even got back to 105. Usually however, I would also have to cross the road to Sammy Bags (as he was known) the greengrocer's for an errand and then call next door to the paper shop to buy the 'Star' which I believed cost a penny.

I would also have to get half an ounce of A1 tobacco for my father and ten Weights or Woodbines being he was a smoker and children as young as I was then, were allowed to buy cigarettes. Next to that was John's and Son's the undertakers who as I recall, had a marble angel in the window. They are still in business today and over the years conducted the funerals of the Herod's and indeed the Warren's.

Chapter Four

Old Jesse still enjoyed his trips to the Buxton Club or sometimes the Walthamstow Dog Track and every Saturday evening he went through the same ritual of getting ready; Mill would be frying his favourite tea of egg, bacon and scallops in a pan of dripping while he had a wash and shave at the kitchen sink. He never took his shirt off but just removed the loose collar that was held in place by a stud at the back and tucked a towel in around his neck. The radio would be on as he eagerly awaited the football results. As soon as the announcer began there would be a lot of shhhhhing and everyone had to be deathly quiet while Jesse, with shaving foam still around his face, checked his coupon. Woe betide anyone who made a sound!

After ripping up his football coupon and throwing it in the fire while mumbling to himself about bloody football players and useless results, he'd finish shaving and then sit down for his tea with a thick slice of crusty bread from Ackers the baker's across the road which had been dipped in the frying pan's juices and fat. Then it was time to put on a clean shirt and collar and pull on his stainless steel expanding shirt bracelets which shortened the length of the sleeves. Finally he would wrap a long white silk scarf that had fringed ends around his neck, put on his coat and trilby and was now ready to go out and meet up with his old cronies, as Mill would call them.

It was on a Sunday after one of these Saturday night sessions that there was an almighty row between him and Mill after she'd gone to the wardrobe and found lipstick on one of his shirts. He swore blind he hadn't been with another woman and Mill accused him of having a carry on with Ester Cohen their next door neighbour who she said was always sweet on Old Jesse. They had a right ol' ding dong until David, their grandson who was living with them at the time, eventually owned up. He had been out on a date with Patsy his future wife to be and had borrowed one of his grandfather's best shirts that had an attached collar and hoped no one would be the wiser. However he hadn't noticed the lipstick when he'd put the shirt back on its hanger in the wardrobe. Thankfully Mill hadn't gone knocking at Ester's door to have it out with her for being the Cohen's were also their landlords, they might have found themselves out on the streets!

In fact it was David who found himself locked out and on the street one night. He would often, although unintentionally, annoy his grandfather by coming home late at night after forgetting his key. Several times he had rung on the front door bell until old Jesse eventually woke up, got himself out of bed and came all the way down the stairs to let him in. Getting fed up with this he warned David that if it happened again he wasn't opening the door so he would have to sleep on the door-step. Of course it did happen again and as much as David rang the bell old Jesse stuck to his word and never came down to unlock the door. Not wanting to sleep on the door step where anyone passing by would see him, he went around the corner into Ringwood Road and down the ally-way that ran along the back of the shops. He climbed up and over the big shed where the wood was stored and jumped down into the back garden. There was a small patch of grass that his grandmother had cultivated which she referred to as 'the lawn' and being it was a warm summer's night he rolled up his jacket to rest his head and decided to sleep there. When he awoke in the morning he wondered at first where he was and then was surprised to find himself in the garden but he was even more surprised to find that during the night someone had covered him over with a blanket! It didn't take a lot of guessing as to who had worried enough about him getting cold but it was certainly a man with a very kind heart. Needless to say, David never forgot his key again.

To hear old Jesse coming in late at night singing his head off with a few verses of, *'There's an ol' mill by the stream....Nellie Dean'* a popular song of the day, was nothing new to the Warren household especially when he'd had a few too many Ben Truman's.

It was after another Saturday night a few days before Christmas that he'd come home singing as usual and as always headed straight to the outside lav. Over his shoulder he carried a large goose, still whole and complete with feathers which he told them (the following day) he'd won in a raffle. Mill was delighted at the sight of the goose because it would be a real treat and with the rib of beef there would be plenty to last the whole week, but she was not delighted at the sight of Jesse who had by now dropped the bird on the kitchen floor and was being sick outside the back door before making his way into the dark lavatory.

The next day having put the goose ready and waiting to be plucked in the cold pantry the night before, Mill cooked the Sunday roast, not the usual rib of beef for she was keeping that to go with the goose being it was for Christmas. So instead there was rabbit with pork strips and a massive Yorkshire pudding and fresh veg. Old Jesse always liked a bit of cold Yorkshire with jam for his Sunday tea after his cockles, whelks and winkles, a typical East End delicacy.

It wasn't until the Sunday meal was almost ready and on the table that she got one of the boys to go upstairs to wake their father.

"Tell him I'm dishing up" she said, "That will get the ol' sod out of bed".

Being they had no inside toilet or indeed a bathroom, Mill kept a very large chamber pot (known as a 'goesunder') under their big double brass bed for them both to use during the night. Old Jesse more so especially after the amount of Ben Truman's he'd knock back and then to bring half of it up back up again wasn't unusual. So like every other morning she had the unpleasant job of emptying the chamber pot into the enamel lidded bucket which was kept in the bedroom especially for that purpose and then carrying it carefully downstairs, emptied the contents down the pan of the outside lavatory.

Now on this particular occasion not only was the chamber-pot full to the brim but so was the bucket and the revolting smell that rose from it was enough to make anyone heave but Mill was well used to it after all those years of living this way. And it would be many more years before she had the luxury of an indoor toilet. However, it took her two trips up and then down the stairs again to complete this unenviable task.

When she was about to empty the first bucket load into the lavatory pan she saw Jesse's false teeth lying in the water smiling up at her and then she noticed on the floor a few shillings in loose change. The coins quickly went into her apron pocket…that was his loss and her gain but as for his teeth, well she thought, 'Sod him and serve him right for coming home drunk again'. So with that thought in mind she emptied the whole bucket load over his teeth without flushing the pan, might as well do it in one go she told herself. She then went back upstairs, tipped the chamber pot into the bucket and that too was subsequently emptied over the dentures. Then she gave the chain a good pull and although she couldn't see them by now, watched as the water flushed the pan clean and waited to see if the teeth had gone. But no, the teeth were still sitting there and so, that's where she left them.

Well, at least that was her intention but when one of the boys exclaimed that they weren't using the lav with their ol' man's teeth looking up at them, she changed her mind and decided she'd better fish them out.

That was of course until old Jesse came downstairs for his dinner. When she heard him coming down she quickly went outside and took the teeth from the window ledge in the lav where she'd put them earlier and dropped them back into the water at the bottom of the pan and hurried back into the kitchen.

"Where's me bleeding teeth?" he mumbled as he came into the scullery cum kitchen looking at Mill who was by now standing by the low brown sink straining steaming cabbage, "You seen 'em?".

"Look down the lav where you left them last night" she replied sarcastically giving a warning look at the others who were sitting waiting at the table trying not to laugh. With that Jesse went outside and after a while they heard the lavatory flushing.

"Blimey, I hope he took them out first" young Jesse said as the others began to laugh.

Then in he came with his teeth in his hand, rinsed them under the cold water tap, put them into his mouth and then sat down to enjoy his dinner! He never ever mentioned this incident and it certainly didn't cause him any harm especially after what had been poured over them but it has certainly caused a lot of amusement over the years whenever the story has been repeated.

Likewise when Mill's chickens got loose and ventured into the house, old Jesse was at the receiving end again, although he never ever knew it.

The back door leading to the garden was open on account of it being a nice day. I called out to tell her that the chickens were in the kitchen. Between us we shooed them out and got them back to their run and put the latch on the door but one was missing. Although we searched the back rooms, along the passage way and into the shop it wasn't to be seen. We even looked upstairs but it wasn't anywhere.

I suggested it may have gone over the fence and into next doors garden.

"I blooming well 'ope not," came the reply "they ain't having one of our Sunday dinners!"

Being these chickens never appeared to lay eggs they were designated for the oven. It was nothing unusual to see a chicken having its neck wrung and being beheaded by one of my uncles who then hung it from a hook to drain the blood and yes, chickens do run around headless but it was the way things were done in those days and no one gave a thought that a young child stood watching. As awful as it now sounds, that's just how it was and I accepted it although my feelings would be completely different now.

The missing chicken was eventually found, sitting on the shelf in the pantry! However, not before it had been pecking at old Jesse's dinner which would be heated up later that evening when he came home from work. The bird was soon returned to its run but what about the dinner?

Mill knew that Jesse wouldn't want it thrown away because he would never let any food be wasted so she turned the liver over where the chicken had been pecking at it and with a fork fluffed the potatoes up a bit more. Poor old Jesse, he never knew a chicken had had a go at his dinner but the rest of us soon did!

Even from an early age I have memories of my wonderful grandparents Mill and Jesse Warren and their furniture shop although my parents, my brother David and I were now living at a place called Priory Court, a large estate where blocks of flats had been built. We had moved there in 1949 but I spent most of my holidays and time at Markhouse Road, mainly I suppose because my mother went out to work.

Prior to this we had been living in Melford Road after leaving Glenthorne Road about the same time as my grandparents had also moved from there. Melford Road was not far from the Buxton Club where Jesse liked to spend most of his Saturday nights when he wasn't at the dogs. However, we were only there a year or so before being given a week's notice prior to being chucked out. This was all down to my mother who had high morals and a very narrow minded outlook on life.

We were living in the upstairs flat of a house at no.19 and the owner, a Mr. Percy Morton lived downstairs. I never knew why my parents had moved there because it meant we had to go through the downstairs rooms where Mr. Morton may have been sitting and through his scullery to use the outside lavatory. Where as in Glenlthorne Road we'd had the whole house to ourselves. Like most terraced or back to back houses of that time there were no bathrooms let alone an indoor lavatory so going through the downstairs flat was acceptable and the arrangement worked. Well, at least it did until one day Mr. Morton brought a lady friend home who moved in with him. When my mother heard about this she was livid. It was sordid and absolute filth she told him. To be living in sin with two young children living above (meaning my brother and I) was downright disgusting and my mother wasn't standing for it… To which Mr Morton told her that if she didn't like it then she could find somewhere else to live and gave her to the end of the week for us all to get out.

I remember that day very well for I recall my mother taking me along with her to a blue telephone box to call the police. Apparently it was to report a man for living with a woman who wasn't his wife! The police were obviously not particularly interested as to what this bloke was up to because by the end of the week we had been put into a Council 'half way house' as it was called. It was a very large house on the edge of Epping Forest where homeless people were put until they could be re- housed. We stayed there living in one room, sharing a kitchen and toilet for around three months before being allocated the newly built flat on the Priory Court estate. We were to live there for the next ten years.

It was from Markhouse Road that over the years I saw my uncles and aunts leave to get married and I was a bridesmaid to three of them. Cissy married Bob (Robert) Ross when I was about 3 or 4 years old but I was considered too young to be a bridesmaid although David being four years older than me was their page boy. They began their married life in Markhouse Road and had the two upstairs back rooms and a section of the wood shed at the bottom of the garden was partitioned off the make a garage for Bob's pride and joy, a Vincent Black Shadow motorbike. Another door was put in the fence so he had access to this garage space via the back ally.

Bob Ross had been a Chief Petty Officer in the Royal Navy during the war and they had married shortly after his return home. When he'd asked Cissy to marry him he made it very clear that he did not want any children and she reluctantly agreed. He was a very strict man and he expected his home and marriage to run as smoothly as the ship of the Royal Navy on which he had served. Meals had to be ready on the dot. The table had to be laid out with neat precision and the cutlery set correctly. A weekly menu had to be observed complete with the appropriate sauces to compliment the meal along with folded table napkins.

Cissy was not allowed to go out to work and would never dream of buying any items for her-self or the home without his approval and he proved to be a very domineering man. The way he is holding her arm in the wedding photo looks like he is keeping her 'under control' and that's just what he did. I recall once she had a beautiful dark red velvet dress made for a special social event they were attending. The dress was made by a local dress maker and three times Bob sent it back for very minor details and faults, e.g. a loose cotton hadn't been trimmed off properly or a slight crease was in the folds, all to be corrected before he gave his approval and settled the dressmaker's bill. He would often speak to Cissy in a very severe fashion which didn't go unnoticed by other family members. Sadly Cissy died some years later of cancer. Bob remarried not long after and became a father to a daughter, something Cissy would have loved to have had but she never found the courage to stand up to this domineering man.

She had married him under his terms and had promised in the eyes off God to love honour and obey. Sadly, I think he used Cissy as a door mat and only married her for his need of a cook and house keeper. There are not many women who would stand for that sort of treatment in today's world but that is how it was and she stood by her marriage vows, till death did them part and she was only in her forties when she died of cancer.

Vera married Walter Simmons who had served out in Africa during the war. He was the son of Mill and Jesse's old friends and neighbours from way back before they had even moved to Walthamstow and had lived opposite them in Glenthorne Road. Walter's father became the Lord Mayor of Walthamstow and it was his influence that helped my parents to come off the waiting list and get the nice new modern flat at Priory Court in 1949. No doubt the five pound back hander must have helped.

When Vera and Walter began their married life together, they lived for some time in the rooms behind Kitty's the cat's meat shop, a few doors along from Mill and old Jesse.

Cissy (Beatrice) Warren and Bob (Robert) Ross's wedding c.1946. To the right of the bride: old Jesse, young Jesse and her mother Mill. Vera was bridesmaid. Jack & young Milly on the far left with their daughter Marion in front. David their son was page boy.

Their only child, a son was born while they were there but it wasn't long before they moved on as no doubt the smell of meat unfit for human consumption may have been just a bit overpowering. Ronnie was the first of Mill and old Jesse's sons to marry. His wife was a beautiful and stunning young woman named Lilly Salmon who had been the winner of several Beauty Queen competitions.

Vera and Walters wedding c.1948.

However, she gave all that up when they married for no doubt Ronnie didn't want his new bride parading in her bathing suit in front of admiring men.

When Ronnie first brought Lilly home to meet the family he introduced her by saying, "Mum, dad, this is Lilly.....Lilly Salmon'

"Nice to meet yer luv, where 'bouts do yer live?"

Before she could answer, young Jesse who happened to be in the kitchen at time, shouted out "In a tin, where else?"

Old Jesse didn't get the joke and later after Ronnie had left to take Lilly home he stroked his chin as in deep thought and said to Mill,

"I think there's something 'fishy' about that girl"

The rest of the family fell about laughing although he didn't seem to realise that his comment about his future daughter-in-law was the cause of their amusement....or did he really know and maybe just kept a straight face?

Young Jesse was the last to marry, he'd met a local girl Jean Foster and they went on to have two children, first a boy and a couple of years later a daughter. Although young Jesse's illness was slowly worsening he never let it stand in his way and tried to lead a normal life as much as possible. Jean had had it explained to her before they married that his disabilities could get worst but no one at the time had any idea just how bad it would become as the years passed. Thankfully despite having this terrible affliction, young Jesse never let his disabilities get him down and he always had a wonderful sense of humour. Jean stood by him throughout their lives together and all credit must go to her for the care, love, help and understanding that she always gave him. Despite the difficulties and no doubt pain that came with this crippling decease Jesse thankfully lived on into his 80's and was blessed with three grandsons.

It was here at Markhouse Road where I would often sit around the open coal fire and listen as my grandparent's told me of their early years and granddad would talk of the Great War while grandma would tell me of the hardships that they had faced and endured. I can still hear my grandfathers voice now, talking about the time he

and young Frank had run back from the advancing Germans, 'There they were' he would say, 'undreds of 'em...all coming towards us....firing their guns...hundreds of 'em....all coming towards us.... we didn't stand a chance....all those poor buggers....shot down they were' he would often give a big sigh and shake his head in disbelief and many a time I saw him wipe away a tear. Then my grandmother whom I always called Nan would say, 'Oh shut up Jesse we've heard it all before' it wasn't that she was un-sympathetic I suppose but probably she knew how upset he could get when he started recalling those horrendous days.

Without my grandparents or the fact that I listened and absorbed every word they said over those years, I would never have written '*FOR THE LOVE OF AMELIA*' nor would I be sitting here today recalling their stories while being a great grandmother myself.

I also have a slight memory of my own great grandmother Sarah Herod although my brother David being four years older than me does remember more. I can recall seeing a very old lady dressed in black from head to toe, sitting in a big chair in the downstairs front parlour of Cranbrook Road and it was said that she even slept in that chair.

I remember she gave me a three penny piece. My brother has since told me that she died in that very same chair and when they removed her to lay her out they were shocked to find an amazing amount of money in notes including the big old white £5 notes under her cushion. Without anyone knowing she must have been hoarding money away for years, which over time had become rather soiled and pongy. However, they were changed at the local bank, despite their unsavoury condition.

I do have very vivid memories of Mill's many brother's and sister's who were my great aunts and uncles and were in my life for many, many years mainly I suppose because they nearly all lived to ripe old ages. It is hard to imagine that Sarah and Joseph's first child (my grandmother) was born in 1888 and their last child died in 2002 (which was Elsie) Therefore their lives spanned from the late 1880's through to the new Millennium.

Jesse and Jean's wedding c.1952

Ron and Lilly's Wedding c.1950

It has given me a great deal of pleasure to be able to recall so much of the life and times of the Warren's and I hope the readers of this book whom I've never met may have got to know Mill and old Jesse Warren as if they too were a part of this family.

Without these two people we, their descendants, wouldn't be here today and it was because of them that I became a genealogist. After their deaths I just had to record everything for the future, it was as if they had wanted me to keep their memories alive. I began my research on the Warren and Herod's ancestry and found a great satisfaction of discovering our families past lives and my love of research began.

Many family members were a great help by giving me even more information but mostly I have my mother Milly to thank and of course the small case full of photo's and documents that my Nan left after she passed away.

Amongst my countless memories I do recall Nan, my grandmother once telling me that if she ever had her life over again she wouldn't want it. In fact she even said, 'I wouldn't even wish my life on my worst enemy'

I must have been in my early twenties at the time and didn't really know why she had said it but if only I'd asked. Even when I grew older I should have asked, something which I now regret because I will never know. What had made her say that? She'd had a most terrible time during the Great War, no money, worrying about her young husband who had signed on without telling her and being on the brink of starvation, so much so that she relied on scraps of food from other people's left over's. Then years later when war was declared yet again she had to live through more horrors as Walthamstow was bombed and all the hardships and fears that war brought with it. There was also the dreadful loss when two of her grandchildren died so young (Millie's children Irene & John) which must have been a most terrible blow for the family.

Then fate struck two more blows when she and old Jesse had tragically lost not one but two daughters, first Vera died and then Cissy both to cancer and that must have been her worst nightmare ever. Vera was just 34 years old leaving behind Walter her husband and her four year old son.

What she'd said about not wishing her life on anyone is now way back in the past and I will never know her true reason for saying what she did. However, she did have a family around her who loved and cared for her deeply but maybe there could never be enough love to make up for the suffering of the past…but I hadn't asked and even if I did, I wonder if she would have told me?

My favourite memories of those years now so long since gone are of the parties and those wonderful Christmas's we all had at Markhouse Road. There always seemed to be so many people in the house, Nan's brother in law Will Gasson who was married to Mill's sister Beatrice carved the goose every year and I remember the large wooden table it sat on. This well used and well scrubbed table in the kitchen had 3 bulbous thick legs but the forth leg was as thin as a walking stick because all the cat's they'd ever owned had been using it for years and years as a scratching post.

The large room over the shop where the knee's ups were held and where someone would soon be playing the piano as everyone began to dance, especially *'Knee's up Mother Brown'* when the floor actually bounced up and down. It was a wonder that the whole floor never gave way sending the piano and everyone else into the shop below. As the floor bounced the piano went with it and slowly it travelled from one end of the room to the other and then slowly back again with pints of beer sloping all over the top of it.

Many years later when Mill and old Jesse did eventually move from Markhouse Road the piano had to be dismantled to get it down the stairs and inside were old cigarette and match boxes, crisp packets, mummified sandwiches plus evidence that mice had been nesting there. That may account for the nights they'd wake up thinking they could hear someone running their fingers along the piano keys...it probably was mice, although neither of them ever ventured from their bed to find out for sure.

However, at these wonderful family 'do's' old Jesse would always get up and do his 'party piece', a popular old song that used to be sung by Albert Clavalier, a Music Hall entertainer way back in the late 1890's. The words old Jesse sang were truly from the heart and always dedicated to Mill and although they often argued, he meant every word;

'We've been together now for forty years
And it don't seem a day too much,
For there ain't a lady living in the land
Who I'd swop for me dear ol' Dutch'

Ron's father- in -law Harry Salmon, would always sing at these 'do's'

'I'll take you home again Kathleen' with such gusto that his face would turn bright red with the exertion and the perspiration would run down his face.

I once overheard my Nan saying that he would burst a blood vessel one of these day and maybe he did, for he died a year or two later.

One of the most exciting things for me at these parties was at bed time when one of my second cousins and I slept in my grandparents big brass bed with its feather mattress and snuggle down under an enormous eiderdown as we watched the light from the coal fire dancing on the ceiling. Above the fireplace a long length of ceiling paper hung like a hammock from one side of the room to the other. Since no one had ever bothered to stick it back up it had, over the years, filled with thick dust and grey fluff. Looking back now it was a real fire hazard but thankfully it never came down and no one ever thought or considered the risks if it had, most likely the whole place would have gone up in smoke. There were no health and safety laws in those days let alone smoke alarms. The only warning you would get was if someone shouted, 'Fire! Fire! Fire!'

Then the following morning especially after a Christmas party and a big fry up for breakfast, all the men would go off to watch Leyton Orient if they were playing at home in Lea Bridge Road and in the evening the partying would start all over again. Mill always thought Friday was the best day for Christmas Day to fall on and her reasoning was pretty sound. If Christmas day fell on a Friday and Boxing Day the Saturday, it gave everyone a chance to get over it on Sunday and they'd be ready to go back to work on the Monday morning. In fact Mill had quite a few amusing sayings. Talking about times past she would say;

"Ah yes, those were the days when bread were a penny a hundredweight and coals a half-penny a loaf." She was referring of course, to the cost of living.

When it came to childbirth, "Well, you've got to get a lot worse before you any get better." She would say.

Teeth; "They are trouble coming and trouble going"

When asked her age she would always reply, "I'm as old as my tongue and a bit older than my teeth"

Peoples looks; "I'd rather kiss a baby's bum then kiss their face"

Getting me to run errands; "You'll have to go dear as I've got a bone in my knee," (I fell for that one for quite a long time).

Advice; "Listen to an old woman who know best", she'd say giving the benefit of her wisdom whether asked for or not.

However, one bit of advice she did give me many years back when my first child was born was I think was very sound. We often hear of cot deaths concerning young babies but I think, like Mill this could be prevented by the following advice; Roll up two small cot blankets, lay the baby on its side and put one rolled blanket in front of the baby against the side of its crib/cot/pram and the other likewise behind the baby's back. This way the baby cannot roll over onto its face and suffocate nor will it be able to roll over onto its back and choke should it be sick. This makes a great deal of sense and I have passed this advice on to many other young mothers over the years including my own daughter.

Another saying she was fond of and I still find myself using it today; if she had her back to someone while in conversation with another person she would turn around and say, 'Sorry I've got my back to yer, but me front's busy' or if someone happened to pass wind she'd say, 'Blimey, what's crawled up your arse and died.' A true lady my dear old Nan! However, she never minced her words and no one was allowed to say, "She' when talking about another woman for Mill would ask, "Who's *she* then, the cat's mother?" We weren't allowed to say that someone had died or was dead, it had to be,' They've passed away'

Then of course while washing us children when we were young we got 'just a cat's lick' as she called it and would always quote, 'Eye's nose, mouth and chin around the corner to uncle Jim' the last bit was of course when we got our necks washed! That's if she remembered that bit.

When she became better off money wise, I recall going with her on a Thursday afternoon to Hackney Wick greyhound racing. If she had a good day and had a win then we'd have a taxi to the top of Markhouse Road but if it had been a bad day and she'd lost, then we'd have to get the bus. Either way, I always got a sixpence (2.5 p) for not telling anyone where we'd been so I always kept her secret and was on a nice little earner myself especially if she did have a good day then I got a shilling (5p) to spend which I would promptly go and spend in Strutt's the candy shop.

For a few years the family business in Markhouse Road did well but then trade slackened off and the two boys had to find work elsewhere. Maybe old Jesse didn't have the head for business because more than once he settled any disputes with customers in the only way he knew how and that was with his fists! Although he was a very kindly man really, it still didn't take much to get his temper flying, a legacy left to him from the horrors he had endured during W.W.1. He would never forget those terrible times and his anger at what he had seen still haunted him. His nightmares were now a thing of the past but his memories had never faded.

On one occasion he had made several glass display cabinets for a retail shop in the local High Street but a few days after they had been collected the man who had bought them wanted his money back. Apparently they had wood worm and obviously unsellable. Old Jesse refused to return the cash and a fight broke out between the two men. It was more than likely that he came out on top and most unlikely that the money was ever returned. It wasn't exactly the correct way of running a business and it was no wonder that trade slackened off.

It was said that old Jesse Warren had once spent a few nights in the local nick for displaying his fighting skills but little is known about this incident although no doubt it could very well be true.

Mill and old Jesse finally decided to close the shop around 1956 but still lived in the premises at the back and in the rooms above. They also painted up the windows to stop passers by looking in. Old Jesse got work with the C.W.S. (Co-op Wholesale Society) using his old skills as a French polisher. He travelled about the South of England or wherever he was needed to re-polish tables and other

244

important pieces of furniture or wall panelling in the Co-op's offices and Board Rooms. It was around this time that Mill had two astonishing surprises, old Jesse had brought Mill home not only a diamond ring but also a gold watch.

He had been working in Bristol and had been away for several days. He's greatest fear he recalled on his return was crossing the Clifton Suspension Bridge. He said he just couldn't do it, a man who had survived the Battle of the Somme could not find the courage to cross this bridge. Whether he did eventually cross it or found another route I cannot now recall. However, on the train returning home he got chatting to another passenger and this man asked him if he was interested in an 18 ct gold watch and a beautiful 5 stone diamond ring that he wanted to sell. Jesse did indeed buy these two items and although he paid £20 for the ring the price of the watch is not known but probably would have only been a few pounds. Mill was delighted with these presents and apart from her wedding ring had never owned anything thing like it in her life. Needless to say, Fish Brothers the pawn shop saw that ring pretty often over the coming years! When I was about 10 years old I remember my grandmother being so upset because she had lost this ring and was terrified as to what old Jesse would say when he knew. Between us we searched and eventually I spotted it resting between the wooden floorboards of the parlour. Oh, how pleased she was and gave me a big hug and then carefully prised the ring out with an old boot button hook. Old Jesse had continued working until retirement age. And he still liked to do a bit of carpentry or polishing so the disused shop which was now only used as a store room for various household items, made an ideal workroom. An old glue pot that had been there for years was often seen bubbling away on a small gas ring. I was always fascinated by the tiny clear golden beads that were added whenever more glue was needed. However, the glue pot had never been cleaned and the outside was caked with hardened glue and it was the same inside and now there was hardly any room for the round almost bristle less brush. Ronnie was working for a Burglar Alarm Company and young Jesse now worked in London. Ronnie was quite pleased to be able to boast that he had fitted alarms in some very influential houses. By now young Jesse's disability was far worse, most of his bones were twisting and his body was distorting but he never let it get him down and continued working until retirement age. He always joked that his life at work was full of ups and downs as indeed it was.........he was the lift attendant at the Evening News offices in London and he always said that the most famous person he took up in the lift was Her Majesty the Queen.

A day at the races. Jesse with Mill to the right.

Marion with son Roy and old Jesse. c.1960

Chapter Five

It was later around 1966 that Mill and old Jesse began to feel the strain of living in such a big house. The stairs were getting far too much for both of them and eventually encouraged by the family, they decided that it was time to find a smaller place to rent.

Over the years various members of the family had lived with them in Markhouse Road, Cissy and Bob had when they were first married and later Ron and Lilly.

Cissy and Bob had been there for a year or and then moved into the upstairs rooms above Mill's sister Beatrice at 4 Story Road just off the High Street (Elsie, another of Mill's sisters lived next door at no. 6).

A few years passed by and because Bob, who was a bus mechanic, had been offered a better job they moved out of the area to a house at Sleets End, Hemel Hempstead where sadly Cissy was diagnosed with cancer. She came home to be with her parents towards the end as was her wish. A renowned faith healer of the time, Harry Edwards, was called to administer his healing powers but it was all in vain and she died in the room above the shop at Markhouse Road.

Ron and Lilly had also lived there for a while after they'd married but had since immigrated to Canada. However, as much as Ron liked the life out there and had a good job, Lilly didn't and so, after a year or two they returned home to England. They then lived for some years in a flat above one of the shops just past the Lighthouse Church in Markhouse Road and their son was born while living there. Later they bought their own house in Nelson Road, Chingford, not far from where Mill and Jesse enjoyed a Saturday night out at the Walthamstow Stadium.

By now Vera and Walter had moved from behind Kitty's the cat's meat shop to an upstairs flat in Clacton Road, still in

Walthamstow and then after another year or two they moved into a Warner's flat in Morieux Road off Lea Bridge Road in Leyton (Warner being the name of the man who had built hundreds of these large houses that were divided into two flats)

Jesse and Jean had bought their own house at Wickford but like Lilly, Jean was homesick and missed her family so they sold that house and moved into a flat at Titney Close, Chingford.

Some years later after Mill and Jesse had passed away, they moved to Thetford in Norfolk where they remained for the rest off their lives.

My parents and I had since moved to Canvey Island in Essex while my brother who was now engaged, stayed with our grandparents. Jack my father who was a window cleaner drove to Walthamstow most week days because that's where his work was and he didn't want to lose the trade he had built up over the years. My mother and I were able to go with him on many occasions to visit Mill and old Jesse and sometimes they came back with us to Canvey Island. One day after a visit to Canvey my mother received a telegram from her mother. It read,

Mill I've left £13 under the carpet in your bedroom STOP. Didn't want dad to know I had it STOP.

We have to remember this was before my parents had a telephone installed and telegrams were the only way to get in touch quickly. However, receiving a telegram did give my mother a bit of a shock but we did have a laugh about it later. Because old Jesse was so tight with his money, Mill always kept everything quiet as to what she did with any money she may have had, the following note she sent me at a later date shows just how true that was;

2 Manor Close
W stew
E17

Dear Marion

Enclose 3 0 0 . 10/- for Debbie
birthday . & 50/- a little towards Ray
glasses. Why I am writing because grand
come to the Phone & I cant mention money (
he thinks we must save I suppose he mean 1
our old age (HA) so you know what to say
to let me know you got it safe.
I cant write any more as grandad is dozing
& may wake up before I finish
        In Haste yours my love to Mum +
            all the Kiddies
            love to you & Ron
            X X X X X X

PS I am sending Debbie card early
you can give it to her on her birthday

The ink is rather faint now on that note written over 40 years ago but reads;

Dear Marion,
Enclosed 3.0.0 (£3) 10/- (50p) for Debbie's birthday & 50/-
(£2.50) towards Roy's glasses. Why I am writing because
Granddad comes to the phone and I can't mention money (as
he thinks we must save, I suppose he means for our old age
(ha) so you know what to say to let me know you got it safe.
I can't write any more as Granddad is asleep & may wake up
before I finish
In haste, give my love to mum & the kiddies,
Love to you & Alec
P.S. I am sending Debbies card early you can give it to her
on her Birthday.

Note; Alec was my late husband of 41 years
Roy is my eldest son and Debbie my daughter.
Since then I had another son, Paul

Although Jesse always had a tendency to be tight with money he was honest and once found an attaché case containing a lot of money which he said amounted to several hundreds of pounds, while he was in the woods with the boys. It had been left by the side of a pond in Epping Forest and instead of keeping it as many would, Jesse noticed a name and address inside the lid of someone living in Chingford.
Hoping to be given a substantial reward, he took a bus ride to Chingford from Walthamstow the following day to return it to the rightful owner. He recalled it was a big 'posh house' and when he explained to the man who opened the door how he had found the money and that he was returning it, the man put his hand in his pocket and said, 'Thanks mate' and gave Jesse half a crown (12.5p today) and closed the door. Jesse

was stunned, he expected at least a 'few quid' for his honesty but after paying out for his return bus fare there was very little profit. He said if he ever found anything like that again he'd keep it but that opportunity never came along.

By now with all their family married and living away from the shop they were on on their own and the place was far too big for the two of them. (I myself had lived there for a year or two after my marriage in 1960) and it was now time for them to downsize.

The local council were very helpful and found them a very nice little one bedroom flat in Manor Close, Manor Road, still in Walthamstow and just off Higham Hill Road.

It was very sad to leave Markhouse Road after all those years but they had so many memories of the place. There had certainly been some very good times there; wonderful parties and four of their children had been married from Markhouse Road. But oh, what heart breaking events happened during those years too. In 1953 the year of Queen Elizabeth's Coronation Mill's mother old Sarah had died in her 84th year. That was to be expected and she had well outlived Mill's father and yes, it was sad that she had gone but what followed the following year was so very, very tragic. Vera their youngest daughter died from ovarian cancer, she was just 34 years old. The whole family were shattered and Vera leaving her four year old son made it even more unbearable. My mother took him into our own home and he became more of a brother to me than a cousin. Then just a few years later as the family had picked the pieces up and put their lives back together; the same tragedy had struck again when their middle daughter Cissy succumbed to the same dreaded cancer. How my dear grandparents came to terms with that I'll never know. To lose one daughter was tragic enough but to lose two daughters was so cruel.

After two or three years, Walter, Vera's husband had remarried and my cousin went to live with his father and step-mother.

However, Mill and old Jesse had settled well into their new home and soon became friendly with the neighbours who lived in the same block. These flats were purpose built for the elderly and having neighbours of the same age made a nice little community.

They would still visit their daughter Milly at Canvey Island for a few days and it was here in July 1975 (5 months before Mill's death) that they both made a tape recording. It had been a lovely day and the family were sitting in the garden. I suggested they recorded any amusing incident that they could recall. Mill spoke of an incident involving her two boys, Jesse & Ronnie as follows;

'When my boys were small' she said, *'I sent them to buy a pound of apples. When they came back I took the apples from the bag and noticed two bites were missing from each apple. Come back here, you two little B's"* (meaning buggers) *I said," Have you been eating my apples?"*

"No mum," Ronnie the youngest replied innocently, "we dropped them and two bits fell out"

Mill laughed as she recalled this story as did the rest of the family and then she added, *"That's the honest truth that is, the little buggers said they'd dropped them"* Then it was time for old Jesse to tell his tale:

"When I was about seven years old," he began, *" I went right up the top of Tower Bridge...right up the top, round and round the stairs to the very top, right up the very top".* He was of course referring to the time when people could go up to the top of the bridge via one of the towers and go across the walkway high above the river and come down the other

side *"When we got to the top,"* he continued, *"there was just me and me mate...right up the top.... and I scratched my initials J.W. so if you ever go up there look for J.W. 'cos that's where I scratched me name, right there, right up the top"*

I still remember the many tales my Nan would tell me of the antics that Ronnie and Jesse got up to; how once when the insurance man called for her weekly payment she'd sent young Ronnie to the door, "Tell him yer mum's out, say I've gone shopping" she'd whispered and off he went to do as his mother bid while she hid behind the kitchen door listening.

"Mum's out" he said as the man stood there with his open book.

"Do you know when she'll be back?"

"Don't know, she's gone up the High Street" he replied remembering what he had been told to say, "She said she's gone shopping".

"Well, did she leave me any money?" the man asked hopefully but knowing it was very unlikely

"I don't know, I'll asked her" Ronnie turned around and shouted down the passage-way,

"Mum, the insurance man wants to know if yer left 'im any money!"

How Mill got out of that one we just don't know!

Then there was the time when a horse got its own back on young Jesse who used to get great amusement by running across Glenthorne Road from one side of the street to other and back again. Each time ducking underneath the milkman's horse. The horse always stood patiently waiting and chewing on the contents of his nose bag as the dairy man delivered milk to the houses along the road. Young Jesse thought this a great game until one day the horse, who'd probably had just about enough of this kid running under him by now, waited until Jesse was just below him and then peed, soaking him through. He went indoor stinking of the horse's urine and crying, "Mum, the horse just wee'd all over me"

Mill told him it served him bloody right and after giving him a clip round the ear she made him have a bath, even though it wasn't Friday, he never played that game again…

Ronnie was often up to mischief too, 'Played up something awful' Mill told me one afternoon as we sat around the fire, all because when he was about six or seven years old, he decided for some reason that he wanted a pony. Every time when he wasn't at school he'd insist on going shopping with her and would drag behind her crying, "I wan' a pony! I wan' a pony!"

"I keep telling yer, they don't sell ponies up the High Street and even if they did, I ain't got the money to buy one"

In the end she got so fed up with it that one day she took him up to a policeman who was standing outside the Fifty Shilling Tailors in the High Street.

"Will you tell my lad that he can't have a pony and to shut up, 'cos he's getting on me nerves."

The copper grinned, winked at Mill and then gave Ronnie a stern look and said,

"Bugger off home lad with 'yer mother and shut up 'cos you ain't having a pony, else I'll arrest yer and send for a Black Maria and they'll take you to cop-shop. Guess they might even put yer in the cells for a few days" he added.

This seemed to do the trick that frightened the life out of Ronnie and he never asked for a pony again.

That incident reminded Mill of another time when she had once left him outside Woolworth's when he was a baby in his pram. She'd been shopping and had gone home but it wasn't until she realised he was missing that she recalled where she had left him! She hurried back to the High Street and there he was, still asleep outside Woolworth's.

Strange, but I do not recall ever hearing any stories of what her three girls, Milly, Cissy and Vera had got up to, it always seemed to be the boys that got themselves into trouble.

However, she did recall a shocking incident that occurred when Cissy was just a few months old; she developed a large swelling on one side of her head. Mill naturally became very worried and took her to the local hospital. A nurse came along and after listening to Mill's account of why she was there, gave one look at the sleeping child and said,

"There's nothing we can do Mother, take your child home, she's dead".

What a terrible thing for her to say and in today's world a nurse be would dismissed and even possibly taken to Court for giving her own diagnosis. Cissy wasn't dead but sleeping and thankfully made a full recovery and the swelling subsided. No one knew what had caused it for it was never investigated because Mill never returned to the hospital.

Another bad incident happened around 1923 which involved young Milly who was about 10 years old at the time.

As she was walking along near St James Street Station one day a large cog flew from the top of a passing tram where the poles were connected to the overhead cables and bounced along the pavement hitting her on the head.

She sustained a pretty bad injury and through it lost many months of schooling for it took a long time for her to make a full recovery.

Both these incidents were just brushed aside by any authorities' because there was not much chance of compensation in those days whereas if it had happened today, things would be very different indeed.

As time passed, old Jesse was beginning to show signs of age. He began to get forgetful and was a terrible strain on Mill but she had stood by him all those long years and wasn't going to let him down now. It was hard for her even though members of the family called in every day to help in anyway they could but Mill still had the burden of making sure he was dressed properly in the mornings, making sure that he had taken his pills and he was subject to terrifying outbursts of temper. He had always had a violent temper which the family knew was due to his terrifying time out in France during the Great War and they were understanding. There had been no such thing as counselling in those days when soldiers returned home suffering from shell shock or stress. He lost his temper if he saw food being left on a plate or even seeing scraps put out for the birds. This would make him very angry but it was indeed understandable knowing how they had been starving in 1915 and his only reason for joining the army was to send money home to feed his family. He had also endured being out in the trenches when food was so very scarce and witnessed the hunger and near starvation for the troops.

Once I recall finding him sitting with his head in his hands at the bottom of the stairs, his thoughts were back to those terrible days. Even after all these years he still had bitter memories. He could never really recall how he'd got back to England but always felt that it was the Catholic priest, Father O'Brien who had helped him.

He often wondered how he'd actually got back from France and had little memory of his return home. He knew there had been terrible pain in his chest and his head had felt like a steel band was getting tighter every day, he knew he had buried his riffle in the sand before getting on a ship because he vowed never to kill another living soul but had little if any, further memory until he found himself in a Manchester hospital.

Thinking back he thought maybe he'd had a heart attack and was shell shocked but it was so many, many years ago now but he had been sent home, he knew that. It saddened him that he never knew what had happened or became of Frank, the young lad who had made it back with him after hiding in the woods as they heard their comrades being shot one by one and then finding the mailbags.

It had been just before Christmas 1916 that he'd come home and now 53 years later he was about to celebrate 58 years of being married to the only woman he had ever loved.
Two days after their 58th Wedding Anniversary in December 1969 a local newspaper did an article on them and asked the secret of a long happy marriage. The reply Mill gave them was far from the truth.

The Guardian and Gazette, December 26th 1969
Give in- and head for happiness

It was a clear cold Christmas when a pretty 21 year old girl emerged from St James Church Walthamstow, a radiant bride. That was in 1911. And on Christmas day this year, Amelia and Jesse Warren of 2 Manor Close, Manor Road will be celebrating 58 years of happiness together. In fact the romance began 60 years ago she was going home for dinner when she bumped into the new lodger. "We just got to know each other," said Amelia "and he asked me to go with him to the Hackney Empire."
Engagement followed and the only problem facing the young couple was the lack of money. With Amelia's 14 brothers and sisters there was no hope of paying for a reception. So they decided to marry on Christmas Day and make that their party. "There was no snow although it was a windy day" says 79 year old Amelia "although we didn't mind the cold. "We have lived through some good times and bad times but we have a lot to be thankful for". One of the bad times was when two of their daughters died of cancer within a few months of each other (This should actually read 'years' not 'months') Helping them celebrate will be their three children, six

grandchildren and three great grandchildren, one of whom is called Jesse to continue the name that has been in the family for generations. And for any young couples planning to wed this Christmas Day Amelia gives this piece of advice; "Give in to each other and don't quarrel and you'll be as happy as we are" Oh dear, if only the readers of that newspaper article had known the truth!

As time passed old Jesse began to hear bells ringing at night and on a couple of occasions threatened to go after his neighbours with a chopper thinking it was them playing tricks on him but of course it was all in his mind, poor soul. There was talk of having him placed in a residential home but Mill was horrified at the thought of that! No, she'd said, they had been married for all those years and she would stand by him until the end. It was her only prayer that when the time came for them to go, he would be taken first because she didn't want him to be a burden on anyone. He was such a lovely man despite his temper and dearly loved Mill and his family but he had no idea of the stress he was causing his wife and of course being concerned for him she got very little sleep.

However, Mill's prayers were not to be answered because at the age of 87 she had a fall and really needed to go into hospital but she still wouldn't leave him and for four days she defied her doctor's wishes until eventually she knew she had to go into hospital because her hip was broken. It was also her dread that if she went into hospital, she'd never come out again and sadly this prediction was to come true.

She had been carrying a meal from the kitchen into her living room where they always ate when she had tripped over a rug and fell.

She was still cooking their meals as she always had done and if she hadn't fallen then I am sure she would have gone on for several more years because her mind and memory were so bright.

She was operated on in Whipps Cross Hospital Leytonstone where she had a successful hip replacement. Meanwhile old Jesse had been taken ill with prostrate problems and he too was admitted to the same hospital but in a different ward on a lower floor. Him being in hospital gave her peace of mind because she knew where he was and knew he was being well cared for and wasn't a burden on the family. By then, young Milly who had long since moved to Canvey Island was staying at her parents flat in Manor Road so that she could visit them both every day as did Ronnie and young Jesse.

She would often take a flask to Manze's Pie Shop in the High Street and get it filled with hot eels and liquor to take into hospital for her mother. This had long since been a favourite of Mill's although now she could only manage to eat very little.

She was very cheerful in herself and talked of plans for when she came out of hospital, I suggested that she got a shopping trolley to make life easier but she was most indignant about that idea, *'Not so likely'* she said *"you won't get me walking up the road like some old lady"* She was 87 at the time!

Mill was taken in a wheelchair to see old Jesse on several occasions but just two weeks before Christmas 1975 she developed pneumonia and it was then that we knew her life was slowly ebbing away. It was so hard for all the family to accept the fact that we were losing her.

A few days before she died I sat beside her bed holding her hand and she was rolling her head from side to side and calling my name, 'Marion, Marion, Marion.' My mother was there too and we didn't know how to help her. Was she in pain? We just didn't know, it was heart-breaking to see her this way and we called for a nurse to make her as comfortable as they could and free her from any pain. If the end was near then please, please don't let her suffer, she didn't deserve that. There was so much I wanted to say to her, I wanted to tell her that I loved her and how dear she was to me but the words did not come for I just felt unable to speak, it was a very heart-breaking time.

I stayed for as long as I could before I had to leave because I had my own children to care for but I could not bear to say goodbye to her. I could not say the word 'Goodbye' knowing it would be for the very last time. I just kissed her and whispered '*Goodnight Nan.*' As I let go of her hand, the hand that had guided me so often through life, I walked away with tears pouring down my face, I could not look back. I knew I would never see her again.

How hard my dear Nan did fight but her body was so tired and she no longer had the strength to carry on. She passed away at 3.30 am on the 28th December 1975 just three days after her 64th Wedding Anniversary.

My mother was at her bedside when the time came and she later told me that Nan had woken up after a long sleep and asked her not to draw the curtains as it was getting dark. The curtains hadn't been drawn but her life was now nearing the end and darkness was engulfing her.

After a while she opened her eyes, looked about as if she was looking for someone and then focused her eyes towards the end of the bed, then with her very last breath said,

"*Hello Mum, what are you doing here?*" Sarah Herod, Mill's own mother had come to take her first born daughter from this world and she died peacefully without any pain, knowing her mother was there waiting for her. What a wonderful way to end her life.

Chapter Six

By now old Jesse was out of hospital and in a nursing home in Leytonstone not far from Walthamstow but he was not happy there and wanted to go back to their old flat in Manor Road but it just wasn't possible. He needed constant care and even on the day of his dear wife's funeral he wasn't well enough to attend.

As much as I loved my grandmother I did not go to her funeral, someone had to be with old Jesse, he couldn't be left on his own while her funeral was taking place so I stayed with him and I felt in my heart that was what she would have wanted me to do.

We sat together on his bed and held hands as we talked about her and I noticed his eyes constantly going to the photo by his bedside of them both sitting together on the wall outside their flat in Manor Road. He held my hand tightly and as he cried, I cried with him. We shared a very precious time together, grandfather and granddaughter, both feeling the heartache and anguish of losing someone so very dear to us both. I had lost my grandmother but he had lost so much more and his pain must have been so much worse then mine. After all those long, long years it would be hard for him to cope, let alone live without *'his dear ol' dutch'*.

Her ashes were laid to rest at Queen's Road Cemetery, Walthamstow along with her two daughters Vera and Cissy and her wishes to have green stone chippings on her grave were carried out, that's all she asked for so as the weeds never grew.

Since those years when she had been a child so much in the world had changed. They had both lived through two World Wars and old Jesse had survived the Battle of the Somme, seen the throne of England change several times, women had got the vote, telephones, television and radio had arrived.

People were able to fly around the world in a matter of hours and man had landed on the moon.

Nan would often remark how easy life was for women today and she was right because she had known hardships during her life that most young women of today could never envisage. How could they ever imagine what it was like to have to boil washing in a copper after filling it with buckets of water and even using an old stone copper where a fire had to be lit underneath as Mill's mother and she had done; to spend all of Monday washing and scrubbing linen and shirts on a glass scrubbing board; drying it around a fire or on lines suspended from the ceilings when the weather was bad. Let alone spending the whole of Tuesday ironing. There were no electric irons; they used heavy irons which were heated on the kitchen range which had to be banked up with coals throughout the day. There was the rationing of food during the war years and queuing for ages to get whatever the shop had had delivered that day. Sometimes they didn't know what they were even queuing for, maybe for eggs or an orange but they still got in the queue. There were no supermarkets as we have today where we can buy anything and anything we want whether we need it or not. So yes, she was right, life was different now for women and indeed she had an answer for everything and was usually right and knew best. *'Listen to an old lady that knows'* she would say and often give advice whether asked for or not but always with the best intentions.

So now I have come to the end of my grandparent's long journey and I hope that someday my own grandchildren and maybe great grandchildren will read about them and perhaps get an insight as to what wonderful people their great, great grandparents were and learn just how life had been for them. I hope too that you the reader will have found this story interesting and feel you have also got to know the Warrens well.

I know that hearts can really ache as mine did at losing my dear Nan whom I'll always love and remember for ever. Of course my grandfather Jesse was very dear to me too but somehow it was my grandmother who played a very important part of my life.

It was 10 months later that granddad Jesse passed away. He had a water   infection and tubes were draining the build up of fluid from his chest. He constantly begged the doctors to remove these tubes. They explained to him what the consequences would be if they were taken away and I am sure he fully understood.

He had no desire to live anymore, life without Mill must have been unbearable and I truly believe his heart was broken. He begged his daughter Milly to take him home with her, he hated the Residential Care Home where he was now living and he hated the hospital. While in the home he had attacked one of the male carers and had him on the floor and even at the age of 86 it had taken two other carers to pull him off. The fighter and survivor in him was still there even in his old age. He wanted Milly to take him home but she had promised her mother as she lay dying that if anything happened to her she would not take on the burden of looking after him and she did not break that promise. He also asked me but I had three young children to care for and sadly just did not have the room.   Old Jesse was never left alone, his two sons and indeed all his family were constant visitors but later the tubes were removed at his own request and he passed away in Whipps Cross Hospital, Leytonstone, on October 27th 1976 aged 86. It was what he wanted and he was at peace. We had now lost them both for they were gone from our lives forever but we found comfort in knowing they were together again just had they had been together for such a long, long lifetime and so it should be, together again, for-ever and always, reunited in death.   After his funeral his ashes were interred with Mill, the woman he had loved for over sixty four years and their two daughters, Vera and Cissy at Queens Road Cemetery, Walthamstow in the town that he had lived in since he came looking for lodgings over 64 long years ago in 1910. After the death of both her parents my mother Milly, wrote the following note as a contribution to this book.

The letter from young Millie reads:

Sunday Nov 9th 1976

I am Milly at the age of 64 years old (nearly) It is impossible to write of all the wonderful things and the sad things in my life.

But the most important thing was that Amelia Charlotte and Jesse Frederick Warren was my Mum and Dad.

Whenever I was in need of help or a friend my mum would know and she would always turn up to be at my side.

Milly inherited her mother's diamond ring that old Jesse had purchased from a stranger many years before when he was on a train and I have her gold watch.
I have since inherited this ring which I shall treasure for always and eventually pass on to my own daughter.

I have now come to the end of my story and to the end of my grandparents' long journey through life. To me my grandmother was a wonderful person and even now as I write I still feel the heartache of losing her and no doubt always will but I have my memories. I am also happy that my own children can recollect memories of her and their great grandfather Jesse Warren.

I began writing this book way back in 1976 after my grandparents passed away but I did not complete the first part of *For The Love of Amelia* until the year 2000 and intended to finish this account soon after. However, time seemed to pass so quickly although over the years I did add a chapter or two but here I am now in 2014 finishing what I started 38 years ago.
It was around this time, just after my grandparents had passed away, that I became a Genealogist. I wanted to record all that my grandmother had told me about her own ancestors which lead to the desire to research even more. Now all these years later, my Family History Folders contain information on every branch of my family, photographs and many various documents.

Since I began writing Part Two of this book my own parents, young Milly as she was always known & my dad Jack Proudfoot have since passed away. My mum was 95 and my dad 98.

When my grandmother took her last breath on this earth she saw her mother Sarah Herod who came for her daughter and so it was that my own mother opened her eyes just hours before she too died and said quite clearly, *'Hello Dad'*. I asked her if she could see him and she replied, 'Yes'. David my brother, my son Roy, daughter Debbie and I sat at her bedside for several hours before she passed away. Although she never regained consciousness we felt at peace because we knew she had seen her own father, old Jesse Warren and we knew he was nearby waiting for her. She died at 9 p.m. on October 26th 2008.

Young Milly had been the first born of Mill and Jesse's five children and she had outlived them all. Her two sisters had died of cancer many years before and both Ronnie and young Jesse had lived to an old age.

I now count my blessings and know how fortunate I have been to have had not only my own parents but also my grandparents in my life for so many, many years.

When family members live to these great ages and then pass away, people will often say, 'Oh, they've had a good innings' but even so, losing them is still hard and we all miss our loved ones dearly. The longer we have them in our own lives, the harder it seems to be when they have to leave us.

Mill and Jesse outside Manor Close, Walthamstow 1975

Elizabeth Amelia Proudfoot
"Milly"

An English Rose
13th January 1913
to
26th October 2008

Eulogy of Mill and Jesse's first born,
young Milly

Mill and Jesse last resting place with their
daughters Vera and Cissy.
Queens Road Cemetery, Walthamstow

I am also very fortunate to have my own wonderful family whom I love dearly and will do so for ever and always.

I hope the memories I leave behind will be as happy as the memories my grandparents and parents left for me.

Marion Cunningham. January 2014